THE RHINE

BORN where blooms the Alpine rose,
	Cradled in the Boden See—
Forth the infant river flows,
	Leaping on in childish glee.
Coming to a riper age,
	He crowns his rocky cup with wine,
And makes a gallant pilgrimage
	To many a ruined tower and shrine.

THE RHINE;

A TOUR

FROM PARIS TO MAYENCE

BY THE WAY OF

AIX-LA-CHAPELLE.

WITH AN ACCOUNT OF ITS LEGENDS, ANTIQ-
UITIES, AND IMPORTANT HISTORI-
CAL EVENTS.

BY VICTOR HUGO.

TRANSLATED BY D. M. AIRD.

University Press of the Pacific
Honolulu, Hawaii

The Rhine:
A Tour from Paris to Mayence
by the Way Aix - La - Chapelle

by
Victor Hugo

ISBN: 0-89875-898-X

University Press of the Pacific
Honolulu, Hawaii
http://www.universitypressofthepacific.com

CONTENTS.

CHAPTER IV.

FROM VILLIERS-COTTERETS TO LA FRONTIERE.

CHAPTER V.

GIVET.

CHAPTER VI.

THE BANKS OF THE MEUSE—DINANT—NAMUR.

A*

CHAPTER XIX.

"FIRE! FIRE!"

CHAPTER XX.

FROM LORCH TO BINGEN.

CHAPTER XXI.

LEGEND OF THE HANDSOME PECOPIN AND THE BEAU-
TIFUL BAULDOUR.

CHAPTER XXII.

BINGEN.

CHAPTER XXIII.

MAYENCE.

CHAPTER XXIV.

FRANKFORT ON THE MAINE.

CHAPTER XXV.

THE RHINE

THE RHINE.

CHAPTER I.

FROM PARIS TO FERTE-SOUS-JOUARRE.

Dammartin : its Literature and Curiosities.—An Accident, and its
Result. — A German Wagon. — The Pleasures of Country
Traveling. — The Philosophical Hunchback and Reasoning
Gendarme. — Meaux and its Curiosities.

ABOUT two days ago I started from Paris.
Pursuing my way by the route of Meaux,
leaving St. Denis and Montmorency on the left,
I cast my eyes upon the rising ground at the
bottom of the plain, but a turning in the road
soon hid it from my sight. On long excursions,
I have a peculiar *penchant* for short stages, hate
to be encumbered with luggage, and love to be
alone in my carriage with the two friends of my
boyhood—Virgil and Tacitus.

As I had traveled by Soissons a few years ago,
I took the Châlons road, which, owing to innova-
tors, or, as they style themselves, utilitarians,
has now but very little interest left. Nanteuil-
le-Haudoin boasts no longer of the castle built
by Francis the First ; the magnificent manor of
the Duke of Valois, at Villiers-Cotterets, has

1

been converted into a poor-house ; and there, as almost everywhere, sculpture and painting—the mind of by-gone ages, the grace of the sixteenth century—have disappeared. The enormous tower of Dammartin, from which Montmartre, nine leagues distant, could be distinctly seen, has been razed to the ground. Its lizard and vertical form gave rise to the proverb, which I could never well understand :

"*Il est comme le château de Dammartin, qui crève de rire.*" [1]

Since it has been deprived of its old *bastille*, in which the Bishop of Meaux, when he quarreled with the Count of Champagne, took refuge with seven of his followers, Dammartin has ceased to engender proverbs. It is now only remarkable for literary compositions similar to this note, which I copied *verbatim* from a book lying on the table of an *auberge :*

" Dammartin (Seine - et - Marne) is a small town, situated on a hill ; lace is the chief article of manufacture. Hotel : *Sainte Anne.* Curiosities : the parish church, hall, 1600 inhabitants."

The short space of time which those tyrants of diligences, called *conducteurs,* allow for dinner, would not permit me to ascertain if it was true

---

[1] He is like Dammartin Castle, bursting with laughter.

that the sixteen hundred inhabitants of Dammartin were really curiosities.

In the most lovely weather, and on the finest road in the world, between Claye and Meaux, the wheel of my vehicle broke. (I am one who always *continues his journey*, for, if the carriage renounce me, I abandon the carriage.) At that instant a small diligence passed, which was that of Touchard. There was only one vacant seat—I took it, and in ten minutes after the accident I was once more on my *route*, perched upon the *imperiale*, between a hunchback and a gendarme.

Behold me now at Ferté-sous-Jouarre, a pretty little town with its three bridges, its old mill supported by five arches in the middle of the river, and its handsome pavilion, of the time of Louis the Thirteenth, which, it is said, belonged to the Duke of Saint-Simon, and is now in the hands of a grocer.

If, in fact, M. de Saint-Simon did possess that old habitation, I very much doubt whether his natal mansion of Ferté-Vidame ever had a more lordly and stately appearance, or was better adapted to his rank of Duke and Peer, than the charming little castle of Ferté-sous-Jouarre.

In traveling, I do not seek for incidents; my desire is fresh scenes, which excite and create ideas, and for that new objects suffice. Besides, I am content with little. If I see trees, the greensward, and have the open air, with a road before and behind me, I am perfectly satisfied. If the country is flat, I like an extended horizon ; if it be mountainous, I like the landscapes, and here one is ever presenting itself to the view. Before me is a charming valley ; to the right and left the strange caprices of the soil—huge hills bearing the marks of husbandry, and squares, pleasing to the sight ; here and there groups of low cottages, whose roofs seem to touch the gound ; at the end of the valley a long line of verdure, with a current of water, which is crossed by a little stone bridge, partly dismantled by age, that serves to unite the two highways. When I was there, a wagon crossed it—an enormous German wagon, swelled, girt, and corded, which had the appearance of the belly of Gargantua, drawn upon four wheels by eight horses. Before me, near the opposite hill, and shining in the rays of the sun, the road takes its course, upon which the shadows of the tall trees represent, in black, a huge comb minus several teeth.

Ah, well! the large trees, the shadow of a comb, at which, perhaps, you are laughing, the wagon, the old bridge, the low cottages—create pleasure, and make me happy. A valley such as this, with a brilliant sun above, always pleases me. I looked around and enjoyed the scene, but my fellow-travelers were constantly yawning.

When the change of horses takes place, everything amuses me. After the cracking of the whip, the noise of the horses' hoofs, and the jingling of the harness, we stop at the door of an *auberge*. A white hen is seen on the highway—a black one amongst the brambles ; a harrow or an old broken wheel in a corner; and children in the height of mirth, with comely, yet far from clean faces, playing round a stack of hay. Above my head is suspended Charles the Fifth, Joseph the Second, or Napoleon — great Emperors, who are now no longer fit for anything but to draw custom to an ale-house ! The inn is full of voices : upon the step of the door the grooms and the kitchen-maids are cracking jokes and composing idyls, while the understrapper is drawing water. Profiting by my high position upon the *imperiale*, I listened to the conversation of the hunchback and the gendarme, then admired the little place, with all its deformities and beauties.

Besides, my gendarme and hunchback were philosophers. There was no pride in them. They chatted familiarly together; the former, without disdaining the hunchback—the latter, without despising the gendarme. The hunchback paid a tax of six francs to Jouarre, the ancient *Jovis ara*, which he explained to the gendarme ; and when he was forced to give a *sous* to

cross the bridge over the Marne, he became en-
raged with the Government. The gendarme
paid no taxes, but related his story with *naiveté.*
In 1814 he fought like a lion at Montmirail: he
was then a *conscrit.* In 1830, in the days of July,
he took fright, and fled: he was then a gendarme.
That surprised *le bossu,* but it did not astonish
me. *Conscrit,* he was only twenty years of age,
poor and brave; gendarme, he had a wife and
children, and a horse of his own; he played the
coward. The same man, nevertheless, but not
the same phase in life. Life is a sort of meat,
which sauce alone renders palatable. No one is
more dauntless than a galley-slave. In this
world, it is not the skin that is prized — it is the
coat. He who has nothing is fearless.

We must also admit that the two epochs were
very different. Whatever is in vogue acts upon
the soldier, as upon all mankind; for the idea
which strikes us, either stimulates or discourages.
In 1830 a revolution broke out—the soldier felt
himself under a load; he was cast down in spirits
by the force of contemplation, which is equal to
the force of circumstances; he was fighting by
the order of a stranger; fighting for shadows
created by a disordered brain—the dream of a
distempered mind—brother against brother—all
France against the Parisians. In 1814, on the
contrary, the *conscrit* struggled with foreign ene-

mies, for things easily comprehended—for himself, for his father, his mother, and his sisters—
for the plow he had just left—for the hut
which he saw smoking in the distance—for the
land which he had trod in infancy—for his suffer-
ing and bleeding country. In 1830 the soldier
knew not what he was fighting for; in 1814 he
he did more than know it—he felt it; he did
more than feel it—he saw it.

Three things very much interested me at
Meaux. To the right, on entering the town, is
a curious gateway leading to an old church—the
cathedral; and behind it an old habitation, half
fortification and flanked with turrets. There is
also a court, into which I boldly entered, where I
perceived an old woman, who was busily knitting. The good dame heeded me not, thus affording me an opportunity of studying a very handsome staircase of stone and wood-work, which,
supported upon two arches, and crowned by a
neat landing, led to an old dwelling. I had not
time to take a sketch, for which I am sorry, as it
was the first staircase of the kind I had ever
seen; it appeared to me to be of the fifteenth
century.

The cathedral is a noble-looking building; its
erection was begun in the fourteenth century,
and continued to the fifteenth. Several repairs
have lately been made. but it is not yet finished,

for, of the two spires projected by the architect, one only is completed ; the other, which has been begun, is hidden under a covering of slate. The middle doorway, and that on the right, are of the fourteenth century ; the one of the left is of the fifteenth. They are all very handsome, though time has left its impress upon their venerable appearance. I tried to decipher the bas-reliefs. The pediment of the left doorway represents the history of John the Baptist ; but the rays of the sun, which fell full on the facade, preventing me from satisfying my curiosity. The interior of the church is superb : upon the choir are large orgees, and at its entry two beautiful altars of the fifteenth century ; but unfortunately, in the true taste of the peasantry, they are daubed over with yellow oil paintings.

To the left of the choir I saw a very pretty marble statue of a warrior of the sixteenth century. It was in a kneeling position, without armor, and had no inscription. Opposite is another ; but this one bears an inscription—and much it requires it, to be able to discover, in the hard and unmeaning marble, the stern countenance of Benigne Bossuet. I saw his episcopal throne, which is of very fine wainscoting, in the style of Louis the Fourteenth ; but, being pressed for time, I was not able to visit his famed cabinet at the Bishop's.

Here is a strange fact. There was a theater at
Meaux before there was one at Paris, which, as is
written in a local manuscript, was constructed in
1547. Pieces of a mysterious nature were represented. A man of the name of Pascalus played
the *Devil*, and afterwards retained the name. In
1562 he delivered the city up to the Huguenots;
and in the year following the Catholics hung
him, partly because he had delivered up the city,
but chiefly on account of his appellation, " *Le
Diable.*" At present there are twenty theaters in
Paris, but there is not a single one here. It is
said that the good people of Meaux boast of this
—which is, to be proud that Meaux is not Paris.

This country abounds with the age of Louis
the Fourteenth—here, the Duke of Saint Simon;
at Meaux, Bossuet; at La Ferté-Milon, Racine;
at Château-Thierry, La Fontaine — all within a
range of twelve miles. The great *seigneur* is
neighbor to the great archbishop, and Tragedy is
elbowing Fable.

On going out of the cathedral, I found that the
sun had hid himself, which circumstance enabled
me to examine the facade. The pediment of the
central doorway is the most curious: the inferior
compartment represents Jeanne, wife of Philippe-
le-Bel, from the *deniers* of whom the church was
built after her death. The Queen of France, her
cathedral in her hand, is represented at the gates

1*

of Paradise; St. Peter has opened the folding-doors to her: behind the Queen is the handsome King Philippe, with a sad and rueful counte-nance. The Queen, who is gorgeously attired and exceedingly well sculptured, points out to St. Peter the *pauvre diable* of a King, and, with a side-look and shrug of the shoulder, seems to say:—

"*Bah!* allow him to pass into the bargain."

CHAPTER II.

MONTMIRAIL.—MONTMORT.—EPERNAY.

Montmirail Castle.—Vaux Champs.—The Recontre and Reflections Thereupon. — Montmort Castle. — Mademoiselle Jeannette —The Churches and the Curiosities of Epernay.—Anecdote of Strozzi and Brisquet.—Henry the Second's Fool.

I HIRED the first carriage I met at Ferté-sous-Jouarre, at the same time asking one question—" Are the wheels in good order?"

On being answered in the affirmative, I set out for Montmirail. There is nothing of interest in this little town, except a pleasing landscape at the end of an avenue, and two beautiful walks bordered with trees; all the buildings, the *Château* excepted, have a paltry and mean appearance.

On Monday, about five o'clock in the evening, I left Montmirail, and, directing my way towards Epernay, was an hour afterwards at Vaux-Champs. A few moments before crossing the far-famed field of battle, I met a cart rather strangely laden; it was drawn by a horse and an ass, and contained pans, kettles, old trunks, straw-bottomed chairs, with a heap of old furniture. In front, in a sort of basket, were three children, almost in a state of nudity; behind, in another, were several hens. The driver wore a *blouse*, was walking, and carried a child on his back; a few steps from him was a woman, bearing a child in her arms. They were all hastening towards Montmirail, as if the great battle of 1814 were on the eve of being fought.

"Yes," I said to myself, "twenty-five years ago, how many poor families were seen flying from place to place!"

I was informed, however, that it was not a removal—it was an expatriation. It was not to Montmirail they were going—it was to America; they were not flying at the sound of the trumpet of war—they were hurrying from misery and starvation. In a word, my dear friend, it was a family of poor Alsacian peasants who were emigrating. They could not obtain a living in their native land, but had been promised one in Ohio. They were leaving their country, ignorant of the sublime and beautiful verses that Virgil had written upon them two thousand years ago.

These poor people were traveling in seeming cheerfulness:—the husband was making a thong for his whip, the wife was singing, and the children playing. The furniture, however, had something about it of wretchedness and of disorder which caused pain; the hens even appeared to me to feel their sad condition.

The indifference of the heads of the family astonished me. I really thought that, in leaving the country in which we first see light, which links our hearts to so many sweet associations, we should, on taking a last look, shed a tear to the memory of the scenes of our childhood—to the land which contained the mouldering ashes of our forefathers: but these people seemed regardless of all this; their minds were set upon the country in which they hoped to obtain a livelihood.

I looked after them for some time. Where was that jolting and tumbling group going?—aye, and where am I going? They came to a turn in the road, and disappeared; for some time I heard the cracking of the whip, and the song of the woman—then all was quiet. A few minutes afterwards I was in the glorious plains where the Emperor had once been. The sun was setting, the trees were casting their long shadows, the furrows which could be traced here and there had a lightish appearance, a bluish mist was at the bottom of the ravine, the fields seemed deserted; nothing could be seen but two or three plows in the distance, which appeared to the eye like huge grasshoppers. To my left was a stone-quarry, where there were large millstones, some white and new, others old and blackened: here, were some lying pell-mell on the ground—there, a few standing erect, like the men of an enormous draught-board when upset.

I determined upon seeing the castle of Montmort, which was about four leagues from Montmiral; I took the Epernay road. There are sixteen tall elms, perhaps the most beautiful in the world, whose foliage hangs over the road and rustles above the head of the passenger. In traveling, there is no tree pleases me so much as the elm; it alone appears fantastical, and laughs at its neighbor, overturning all as it bends its head, and making all kinds of grimaces to the passers-by in the evening. The foliage of the young elm may be said to spring forth when your eyes are fixed upon it. From Ferté to the place where the sixteen elms are seen, the road is bordered only with poplars, aspens, and walnut-trees, which circumstance did not at all please me.

The country is flat, the plain extending far beyond the range of the eye. Suddenly, on leav-a group of trees, we see on the right, half hidden in a declivity, a number of turrets, weather-cocks, and housetops—it is the castle of Montmort.

My cabriolet stopped, and I alighted before the door of the castle. It is an exquisite fortress of the sixteenth century, built of brick. with slate-work: it has a double *enciente*, a moat, a three-arched bridge, and a village at its foot: all around is pleasant, and the castle commands a most extensive view. It has a winding staircase for men, and a *rampe* for horses. Below, there is also an old iron door, which leads to the embrasures of the tower, where I saw four small engines of the fifteenth century. The garrison of the fortress at present consists of an old servant, Mademoiselle Jeannette, who received me with the greatest civility. Of the apartments of the interior, there only remain a kitchen, a very fine vaulted room with a large mantelpiece, the great hall (which is now made a billiard-room), and a charming little *cabinet*, with gilt wainscoting. The great hall is a magnificent chamber: the ceiling, with its beams painted, gilded, and sculptured, is still entire; the mantelpiece, surmounted by two noble-looking statues, is of the finest style of Henry the Third. The walls were in former times covered with vast squares of tapestry, on which were the portraits of the family. At the revolution a few daring individuals of the neighboring village tore down the tapestries and burned them, which was a fatal blow to feudalism; the proprietor replaced them with old engravings, representing views of Rome and of the battles of the great Condé. On leaving, I gave thirty sous to Mademoiselle Jeannette, who was bewildered with my bounty.

Night was coming on when I left Montmort.

The road is one of the most detestable in the world. It leads into a wood which I entered, and consequently I saw nothing of Epernay but colliers' huts, the smoke of which was forcing its way among the branches of the trees; the red mouth of a distant furnace appeared for a few moments, and the whistling wind agitated the leaves around. Above my head, in the heavens, the splendid chariot was making its voyage in the midst of stars, while my poor *patache* was jogging along among pebbles.

Epernay—yes, it is the town for Champagne; —nothing more, nothing less.

Three churches have succeeded each other; the first, a Roman church, was built in 1037, by Thibaut the First Count of Champagne, and son of Eudes; the second, a church of the *Renaissance*, was built in 1540, by Pierre Strozzi, Marshal of France, Seigneur d'Epernay, who was killed at the seige of Thionville, in 1558; the third, the present one, appeared to me to be built from the design of Monsieur Poterlet-Galichet, a worthy merchant, whose shop and name are close to the church. All three are admirably described and summed up by these names: Thibaut the First, Count of Champagne; Pierre Strozzi, Marshal of France; and Poterlet-Galichet, grocer.

To tell you the truth, the last-mentioned

church is a hideous building, plastered white, and has a heavy appearance, with triglyphs supporting the architrave. There is nothing left of the first church; and of the second, but a few large stained windows, and an exquisite facade. One of the windows gives the history of Noah with great *naiveté*. The window-frames and facade are daubed with the hideous plaster of the new church. It seemed to me as if I saw Odry, with his short white trousers, his blue stockings, and his large shirt-collar, carrying the *casque* and cuirass of Francis the First.

They wished to show me the curiosity of the country—a great wine-cellar, which contains one hundred thousand bottles. On my way I came in sight of a field of turnips, where poppies were in flower and butterflies sporting in the rays of the sun. I went no further—the great cave could well spare my visit.

I forgot to mention that Thibaut the First was interred in his church, and Strozzi in his; however, I should decidedly disapprove of M. Poterlet-Galichet having a place in the present one.

Strozzi was rather what may be termed a *brave* man. Brisquet, the Fool of Henry the Second, amusing himself one day, greased, before the whole court, a very handsome cloak that the marshal had put on for the first time. This excited much laughter, and Strozzi resorted to a most cruel revenge. For me, I would not have laughed, nor would I have avenged myself. To bedaub a velvet coat with grease!—I have never been over-delighted with this pleasantry of the sixteenth century.

CHAPTER III.

CHALONS.—SAINTE MENEHOULD.—VARENNES.

The Reverie.—The Arrest of Louis the Sixteenth.—The Salutation and its Effects.—Notre Dame at Chalons.—Antiquarian
Forgetfulness. — The Inscription. — Watchman, Wife, and
Gnome Son.—Abbey of Notre Dame de l'Epine.—Storm.—
Metz Hotel.—Sleeping Canary.—Host and Hostess.—Champagne and the Signification of Champenois.—Madame Sablière and La Fontaine.

YESTERDAY, at the decline of day, while
my *cabriolet* was rapidly rolling by Sainte
Menehould, I was reading these sublime and
beautiful lines :

"Mugitusque bovum mollesque sub arbore somni.

*   *   *   *   *   *

Speluncæ vivique lacus."

For some time, I rested my hand upon my
book, with a soul full of those vague ideas—sad,
yet sweet—which the rays of a setting sun generally awaken in my mind, when the noise of the
carriage-wheels on the causeway awoke me from
my reverie. We were entering a town ; but what
town was it ? The coachman's reply, " Varennes." We traversed a street which had something grave and melancholy in its appearance ;
the doors and shutters of the houses were closed,
and grass was growing in the courts. Suddenly,

after having passed an old gateway of the time of Louis the Thirteenth, we entered a square, surrounded with small white houses, of one story high. Louis the Sixteenth, on his flight in 1791, was arrested in this square by Drouet, the post-master of Sainte Menehould. There was then no post at Varennes. I descended from my carriage, and for some time kept looking at this little square, which, to the man who does not think of past events, has a dull appearance ; but to him who does, it has a sinister one. It is reported here that Louis, when arrested, protested so strongly that he was not the King (what Charles the First would never have done), that the people, half inclined to credit his statement, were about to release him, when a Monsieur Ethé, who had a secret hatred against the court, appeared. This person, like a Judas Iscariot, said to the King :

"Good day, Sire."

This was enough. The King was seized. There were five of the royal family in the carriage with him ; and the *misérable*, with these words, effected their downfall.

"*Bon jour, Sire,*" was for Louis the Sixteenth, for Marie Antoinette, and for Madame Elizabeth, the guillotine ; for the Dauphin, the torture of the Temple ; and for Madame Royale, exile and the extermination of her race.

Varennes is about fifteen leagues from Rheims
—that is to say, for my coachman; to the mind
there is an abyss—the Revolution.

I put up for the night at a very ancient-
looking *auberge*, which had the portrait of Louis
Philippe above the door, with the words in-
scribed :

"Au Grand Monarque."

During the last hundred years, Louis the Fifteenth, Buonaparte, and Charles the Tenth, had
each figured in his turn. Louis the Sixteenth
was, perhaps, arrested at the *Grand Monarque*,
and, on looking up, saw the portrait of himself—
Pauvre Grand Monarque !

This morning I took a walk into the town,
which is very pleasantly situated on the banks
of a very pretty river. The old houses of the
high town, seen from the right bank, form a very
picturesque ampitheater ; but the church, which
is in the low town, is truly insignificant. It is
within sight of my inn, and I can see it from the
table at which I write. The steeple is dated 1766,
exactly a year before Madame Royale was born.

I visited the church ; and if I did not find all I
expected, I found what I did not expect—that
is, a very pretty Notre Dame at Chalons. What
have the antiquaries been thinking of, when,
speaking of Sainte Etienne, they never breathed
a word about Notre Dame ? The Notre Dame

of Chalons is a Roman church, with arched roofs, and a superb spire bearing the date of the fourteenth century. In the middle is a lantern crowned with small pinions. A beautiful *coup d'œil* is afforded here (a pleasure which I enjoyed) of the town, the Marne, and the surrounding hills. The traveler may also admire the splendid windows of Notre Dame, and a rich *portail* of the thirteenth century. In 1793 the people of this place broke the windows and pulled down the statues ; they also destroyed the lateral gateway of the cathedral, and all the sculpture that was within their reach. Notre Dame had four spires, three of which are demolished, testifying the height of stupidity, which is nowhere so evident as here. The French Revolution was a terrible one ; the revolution *Champenoise* was attended with acts of the greatest folly.

On the lantern I found engraved the inscription, apparently in the writing of the sixteenth century :

"Le 28 Aout, 1508, la paix a été publiée à Chal. . ."

This inscription, which is partly defaced, and which no one has sought to decipher, is all that remains of that great political act—the conclusion of peace between Henry the Third and the Huguenots, by the intercession of the Duke of Anjou, previously the Duke of Alençon. The

Duke of Anjou was the King's brother, and had an eye upon the Pays Bas, and pretensions to the hand of Elizabeth of England; but the war with the religious sects which succeeded thwarted him in his plans. The peace, that happy event, proclaimed at Chalons in 1580, was forgotten by the whole world on the 22nd of July, 1839.

The person who conducted me to this lantern was the watchman of the town, who passed his life in the *guette*, a little box with four small windows. His box and ladder are to him a universe; he is the eye of the town, always open, always awake. Perpetual *insomnia* would be *somewhat* impossible. True, his wife helps him. Every night at twelve o'clock he goes to sleep and she goes to watch; at noon they again change places—thus performing their rounds at each other's side without coming in contact, except for a minute at noon and another at midnight. A little gnome, rather comically shaped, whom they call their son, is the result of the *tangent*.

There are three churches at Chalons:—St. Alpin, St. Jean, and St. Loup.

About two leagues from Chalons, upon the St. Menehould road, the magnificent Abbey of Notre Dame de l'Epine suddenly presents itself. I remained upwards of two hours in this church, rambling round and round. The wind was blowing strongly. I held my hat with both hands, and stood, my eyes filled with dust, admiring the beauties of the edifice.

I continued my route, and after traveling three miles came to a village where the inhabitants were celebrating, with music and dancing, the fete of the place. On leaving, I perceived, on the summit of a hill, a mean-looking white house, upon the top of which was a telescope, shaped like an enormous black insect, corresponding with Notre Dame de l'Epine.

The sun was setting, the twilight approaching, and the sky cloudy; from the plain I looked at the hills, which were half covered with heath, like a *camail d'éveque*, and, on turning my head, saw a flock of geese that were cackling joyously.

"We are going to have rain," the coachman said.

I looked up—the half of the western sky was shrouded in an immense black cloud; the wind became boisterous; the hemlock in flower was leveled with the ground; and the trees seemed to speak in a voice of terror. A few moments expired—the rain poured down in torrents; and all was darkness, save a beam of light which escaped from the declining sun. There was not a creature to be heard or seen—neither man upon the road, nor bird in the air. Loud peals of thunder shook the heavens. and brilliant flashes of lightning contrasted wildly with the prevailing darkness.

A blast of wind at length dispersed the clouds towards the east, and the sky became pure and calm.

On arriving at Sainte Menehould the stars were shining brightly. This is a picturesque little town, with its houses built at random upon the summit of a green hill, and surmounted by tall trees. I saw one thing worthy of remark at Sainte Menehould—that is, the kitchen at the hotel of Metz. It may well be termed a kitchen : one of the walls is covered with pans, the other with crockery; in the middle, opposite the window, is a splendid fire and an enormous chimney; all kinds of baskets and lamps hang from the ceiling; by the chimney are the jacks, spits, pot-hangers, kettles, and pans of all forms and sizes; the shining hearth reflects light in all corners of the room, throwing a rosy hue on the crockery, causing the edifice of copper to shine like a wall of brass, while the ceiling is crowded with fantastic shadows. If I were a Homer or a Rabelais, I would say :

" That kitchen is a world, and the fireplace is its sun."

It is indeed a world—a republic—consisting of men, women and children ; male and female servants, scullions, and waiters ; frying-pans over

2

chafing dishes, bounded by pots and kettles; children playing, cats and dogs mewing and barking, with the master overlooking all;—*mens agit at molem.* In a corner is a clock, which gravely warns the occupants that time is ever on the wing.

Among the innumerable things which hung from the ceiling, there was one that interested me more than all the others—a small cage, in which a canary was sleeping. The poor creature seemed to me to be a most admirable emblem of confidence; notwithstanding the unwholesomeness of the den, the furnace, the frightful kitchen, which is day and night filled with uproar, the bird sleeps. A noise, indeed, is made around it —the men swear, the women quarrel, the children cry, the dogs bark, the cats mew, the clock strikes, the water-cock spouts, the bottles burst, the diligences pass under the arched roof, making a noise like thunder—yet the eyelid of the feathered inhabitants move not.

Apropos, I must declare that people generally speak too harshly of inns, and I myself have often been the first to do so. An *auberge,* take it all in all, is a very good thing, and we are often very glad to find one. Besides, I have often remarked that there is almost in all *auberges* an agreeable landlady; as for the host, let turbulent travelers have him—give me the hostess. The former is a being of a morose and disagreeable nature, the latter cheerful and amiable. Poor woman! sometimes she is old, sometimes in bad health, and very often exceedingly bulky. She comes and goes; is here and there—this moment at the heels of the servants, the next one chasing the dogs; she compliments the travelers, frowns at the head servant; smiles to one, scolds another; stirs the fire; takes up this and sends away that; in fact, she is the soul of that great body called an *auberge*, the host being fit for nothing but drinking in a corner with wagoners. The fair hostess of La Ville de Metz, at St. Menehould, is a young woman about sixteen years of age, is exceedingly active, and she conducts her household affairs with the greatest regularity and precision. The host, her father, is an exception to the general run of inn-keepers, being a very intelligent and worthy man; in all, this is an excellent *auberge*.

I left St. Menehould, and pursued my way to Clermont. The road between those two towns is charming; on both sides is a forest of trees, whose green leaves glitter in the sun, and cast their detached and irregular shadows on the highway. The villages have something about them of a Swiss and German appearance—white stone houses, with large slate roofs projecting three or four feet from the wall. I felt that I was in the neighborhood of mountains: the Ardennes, in fact, are here.

Before arriving at Clermont we pass an admirable valley, where the Marne and the Meuse meet. The road is betwixt two hills, and is so steep that we see nothing before us but an abyss of foliage.

Clermont is a very handsome village, headed by a church, and surrounded with verdure.

I find that I have made use of the word *Champenois*, which, by some proverbial acceptation, is somewhat ironical; you must not mistake the sense which I affix to it. The proverb —more familiar, perhaps, than it is applicable— speaks of Champagne as Madame la Sablière spoke of La Fontaine—" That he was a man of *stupid* genius,"—which expression is applied to a genius of *Champagne.* That, however, neither prevents La Fontaine from being an admirable poet, nor Champagne from being a noble and illustrious country. Virgil might have spoken of it. as he did of Italy—

> " Alma parens frugum,
> Alma virum."

Champagne is the birthplace, the country of Amyot—that *bonhomme* who took up the theme of Plutarch, as La Fontaine did that of Æsop; of Thibaut the Fourth, who boasted of nothing more than being the father of Saint Louis; of

Charlier de Gerson, who was chancellor of the
university of Paris ; of Amadis, Jamyn, Colbert,
Diderot ; of two painters, Lantare and Valentin ;
of two sculptors, Girardon and Bouchardon ; of
two historians, Flodoard and Mabillon ; of two
cardinals full of genius, Henry de Lorraine and
Paul de Gondi : of two popes full of virtue,
Martin the Fourth and Urban the Fourth ; of a
king full of glory, Philippe-Auguste.

Champagne is a powerful province, and there
is no town or village in it that has not something
remarkable. Rheims, which owns the cathedral
of cathedrals, was the place where Clovis was
baptized. It was at Andelot that the interview
between Gontran King of Bourgogne, and Childe-
bert King of Austrasie, took place. Hinemar
took refuge at Epernay, Abailard at Provim,
Héloise at Paraclet. The Gordiens triumphed
at Langres, and in the middle age its citizens
destroyed the seven formidable castles—Chagney,
Saint Broing, Neuilly Cotton, Cobons, Bourg,
Humes, and Pailly. The league was concluded
at Joinville in 1584 ; Henry the Fourth was pro-
tected at Chalons in 1591 ; the Prince of Orange
was killed at Saint Dizier ; Sezenne is the ancient
place of arms of the Dukes of Bourgogne ; Ligny
l'Abbaye was founded in the domains of Seigneur
Chatillon, by Saint Bernard, who promised the
seigneur as many perches of land in heaven as

the sire had given him upon earth. Mouzon is the fief of the Abbot of Saint Hubert, who sends six coursing dogs, and the same number of birds of prey, every year to the King of France.

Champagne retains the *empreinte* of our ancient kings—Charles' the Simple for the *sirerie* at Attigny; Saint Louis and Louis the Fourteenth, the devout king and the great king, first lifted arms in Champagne; the former in 1228, when raising the siege of Troyes—the latter in 1652, at Sainte Menehould.

The ancient annals of Champagne are not less glorious than the modern. The country is full of sweet *souvenirs*—Merovée and the Francs, Actius, and the Romans, Theodoric and the Visigoths, Mount Jules and the tomb of Jovinus. Antiquity here lives, speaks, and cries out to the traveller, " *Sta, viator !* "

From the days of the Romans to the present day, the town of Champagne, surrounded at times by the Alains, the Suèves, the Vandals, and the Germans, would have been burnt to the ground, rather than have been given over to the enemy. They are built upon rocks, and have taken for their device " *Donec moveantur.*"

In 451 the Huns were destroyed in the plains of Champagne; in 1814, if God had willed it, the Russians would also have met the same fate.

Never speak of this province but with respect.

How many of its children have been sacrificed for France! In 1813 the population of one district of Marne consisted of 311,000. In 1830 it had only 309,000; showing that fifteen years of peace had not repaired the loss.

But, to the explanation : When any one applies the word *bete* to Champagne, change the meaning : it signifies *naïf*, simple, rude, primitive, and redoubtable in need. A *bete* may be a lion, or an eagle. It is what Champagne was in 1814.

CHAPTER IV.

FROM VILLERS-COTTERETS TO LA FRONTIERE.

The Effects of Traveling.—The Retrograde Movement.—Reflection.—The Secret of Stars.—The Inscription " I. C."—The
Cathedral where King Pepin was Crowned.—The Prisoner's
sad Rencontre.—Rheims.—Church at Mezieres.—The Effects
of a Bomb. — Sedan and its Contents. — The Transpiring
Events at Turenne's Birth.—Conversation of a Sir John Falstaff and his Better Half.

I ARRIVED at Givet at four o'clock in the
morning, bruised by the jolting of a fright-
fnl vehicle, which the people here call a diligence. I stretched myself, dressed as I was,
upon a bed, fell asleep, and awoke two hours
afterwards. On opening the window of my
chamber, with the idea of enjoying the view
which it might afford, the only objects which
caught my attention were the angle of a little
white cottage, a water-spout, and the wheel of a
cart. As for my room, it is an immense hall,
ornamented with no less than four beds.

A trifling incident, not worth relating, caused
me to make a retrograde movement from Varennes to Villers-Cotterets; and the day before
yesterday, in order to make up for lost time, I
took the diligence for Soissons. There was no

passenger but myself, a circumstance which was in no way disconcerting, as it gave me an opportunity of turning over at my ease the pages of some of my favorite authors.

As I approached Soissons, day was fast fading, and night had cast its sombre aspect over that beautiful valley where the road, after passing the the hamlet of La Felie, gradually descends, and leads to the cathedral of Saint-Jean-des-Vignes. Notwithstanding the fog which rose around, I perceived the walls and roofs of the houses of Soissons, with a half-moon peering from behind them. I alighted, and, with a heart fully acknowledging the sublimity of nature, gazed upon the imposing scene. A grasshopper was chirping in the neighboring field; the trees by the road-side were softly rustling; and I saw, with the mind's eye, Peace hovering over the plain, now solitary and tranquil, where Cæsar had conquered, Clovis had exercised his authority, and where Napoleon had all but fallen. It shows that men—even Cæsar, Clovis, and Napoleon—are only passing shadows; and that war is a fantasy which terminates with them; whilst God —and Nature, which comes from God—and Peace, which comes from Nature—are things of eternity.

Determined on taking the Sédan mail, which does not arrive at Soissons till midnight, I allowed

2*

the diligence to proceed, knowing that I had
plenty of time before me. The *trajet* which
separated me from Soissons was only a charming
promenade. When a short distance from the
town, I sat down near a very pretty little house,
upon which the forge of a blacksmith shed a
faint light. I looked upwards: the heavens were
serene and beautiful; and the planets—Jupiter,
Mars, and Saturn—were shining in the south-
east. The first, whose course for three months
is somewhat complicated, was between the other
two, and was forming a perfectly straight line.
More to the east was Mars, fiery in his appearance, and imitating the starry constellation by
a kind of *flamboiement farouche.* A little above,
shining softly, and with a white and peaceful appearance, was that monster-planet—the frightful
and mysterious world—which we call Saturn. On
the other side, at the extremity of the view, a
magnificent beacon reflected its light on the
sombre hills which separate Noyon from Soisson-
nais. As I was asking myself the utility of such
a light in these immense plains, I saw it leaving
the border of the hills, bounding through the
fog, and mounting near the zenith. That beacon
was Aldebaran, the three-colored sun, the enormous purple, silvery, and blue star, which rises
majestically in the waste of the crepuscule.

O what a secret there is in these stars! The

poetical, the thinking, and the imaginative, have, in turn, contemplated, studied, and admired them : some, like Zoroaster, in bewilderment—others, like Pythagoras, with inexpressible awe. Seth named the stars, as Adam did animals. The Chaldeans and the Genethliaques, Esdras and Zorobabel, Orpheus and Homer, Pherecide, Xenophon, Hecatæus, Herodotus, and Thucydides—all eyes of the earth, so long shut, so long deprived of light—have been fixed from one age to another on those orbs of heaven which are always open, always lighted up, always living. The same planets, the same stars, that fix our attention to-night, have been gazed at by all these men. Job speaks of Orion and of the Pleiades ; Plato listened and distinctly heard the vague music of the spheres ; Pliny thought that the sun was God, and that the spots on the moon were the exhalations of the earth. The poets of Tartary named the pole *senisticol*, which means an *iron nail ;* Rocoles says, " That the *lion* might as well have been called the *ape ;*" Pacuvius would not credit astrologers, under the idea that they would be equal to Jupiter :

> " Nam si qui, quæ eventura sunt, prævideant,
> Æquiparent Jovi."

Favorinus asked himself this question :—" Si vitæ mortisque hominum rerumque numanarum omnium et ratio et causa in cœlo et apud *stellas foret?*" Aulus-Gellius, sailing from Egine to Pirée, sat all night upon the poop, contemplating the stars. "*Nox fuit clemens mare, et anni æstas cœlumque liquide serenum : sedebamus ergo in puppi simul universi et lucentia sidera consider-abamus.*" Horace himself—that practical phi-losopher—the Voltaire of the age of Augustus—greater poet, it is true, than the Voltaire of Louis the Fifteenth—shuddered when looking at the stars, and wrote these terrible lines :—

> "Hunc solem, et stellas et decedentia certis,
> Tempora momentis sunt qui formidine nulla
> Imbuti spectant."

As for me, I do not fear the stars—I love them : still, I have never reflected without a certain con-viction that the normal position of the heavens is night; and what we call "day," arises from the appearance of a bright illuminary.

We cannot always be looking at immensity; ecstasy is akin to prayer; the latter breathes consolation, but the former fatigues and ener-vates. On taking mine eyes from above, I cast them upon the wall facing me; and even there subject was afforded for meditation and thought. On it were traces, almost entirely effaced, of an ancient inscription. I could only make out I. C. Without doubt, they referred either to Pagan or Christian Rome—to the city of strength, or to

that of faith. I remained—my eyes fixed upon
the stone, which seemed to become animate—
lost in vain hypotheses. When I. C. were first
known to men, they governed the world; the
second time, they enlightened it—Julius Cæsar
and Jesus Christ.

Dante, on putting Brutus the murderer, and
Judas the traitor, together in the lowest extremity of hell, and causing them to be devoured
by Satan, must have been influenced by a similar
thought to that which engrossed my whole attention.

Three cities are now added to Soissons—the
Noviodunum of the Gauls, the Augusta Suessonium of the Romans, and the old Soissons of
Clovis, of Charles the Simple, and of the Duke
of Mayenne. Nothing now remains of Suessonium but a few ruins; among others, the ancient
temple, which has been converted into the chapel
of Saint Pierre. Old Soissons is more fortunate,
for it still possesses Saint-Jean-des-Vignes, its
ancient castle, and the cathedral where Pepin
was crowned in 752.

It was very dark when I entered Soissons;
therefore, instead of looking for Noviodonum or
Suessonium, I regaled myself with a tolerably
good supper. Being refreshed, I went out and
wandered about the gigantic *silhouette* of Saint-
Jean-des-Vignes, and it was twelve o'clock before

I returned to the *auberge*, when silence and darkness prevailed.

Suddenly, however, a noise broke upon my ear; it was the arrival of the mail-coach, which stopped a few paces from the inn. There was only one vacant place, which I took; and was on the point of installing myself, when a strange uproar—cries of women, noise of wheels, and trampling of horses—broke out in a dark narrow street adjoining. Although the driver stated that he would leave in five minutes, I hurried to the spot; and on entering the little street, saw, at the base of a huge wall, which had the odious and chilling aspect peculiar to prisons, a low arched door, that was open. A few paces farther on, a mournful-looking vehicle, stationed between two gendarmes on horseback, was half hid in the obscurity; and near the wicket four or five men were struggling and endeavoring to force a woman, who was screaming fearfully, into the carriage. The dim light of a lantern, which was carried by an old man, cast a lugubrious glare upon the scene. The female, a robust countrywoman about thirty years of age, was fiercely struggling with the men—striking, scratching, and shrieking; and when the lamp shone upon the wild countenance and disheveled hair of the poor creature, it disclosed, melancholy to behold, a striking picture of despair. She at last seized one of the iron bars of the wicket ; but the men, with a violent effort, forced her from it, and carried her to the cart. This vehicle, upon which the lantern was then shining, had no windows, small holes drilled in front supplied their place. There was a door at the back part, which was shut, and guarded by large bolts of iron. When opened, the interior of the *carriole* disclosed a sort of box, without light, almost without air. It was divided into oblong compartments by a thick board, the one having no communication with the other, and the door shutting both at the same time. One of the cells, that to the left, was empty, but the right one was occupied. In the angle, squatted like a wild beast, was a man—if a kind of spectre, with a broad face, a flat head, large temples, grizzled hair, short legs, and dressed in a pair of old, torn trousers and tattered coat, may be called one. The legs of the wretched man were closely chained together ; a shoe was on his right foot, while his left, which was enveloped in linen stained with blood, was partly exposed to view. This creature, hideous to the sight, who was eating a piece of black bread, paid no attention to what was going on around him ; nor did he look up to see the wretched companion that was brought him. The poor woman was still struggling with the men, who were endeavoring to thrust her into the empty cell, and was crying out, " No, I shall not ! Never—never !—kill me sooner—never ! "

In one of her convulsions she cast her eyes into the vehicle, and on perceiving the prisoner she suddenly ceased crying, her legs trembled, her whole frame shook, and she exclaimed, with a stifled voice, but with an expression of anguish that I shall never forget :

" Oh, that man ! "

The prisoner looked at her with a confused yet ferocious air. I could resist no longer. It was clear that she had committed some serious crime —perhaps robbery, perhaps worse ; that the gendarmes were transporting her from one place to another in one of those odious vehicles metaphorically called by the *gamins* of Paris "*paniers à salade ;*" but she was a woman, and I thought it my duty to interfere. I called to the galley-sergeant, but he paid no attention to me. A *worthy* gendarme, however, stepped forward, and, proud of his little authority, demanded my passport. Unfortunately I had just locked up that *essentiel* in my trunk, and, whilst entering into explanations, the jailers made a powerful effort, plunged the woman half-dead into the cart, shut the door, pushed the bolts, and when I turned round all had left, and nothing was heard but the rattling of the wheels and the trampling of the escort.

A few minutes afterwards I was comfortably seated in a carriage drawn by four excellent horses. I thought of the wretched woman, and I contrasted, with an aching heart, my situation with hers. In the midst of such thoughts I fell asleep.

When I awoke, morning was breaking; we were in a beautiful valley—that of Braine-sur-Vesle. Venus was shining above our heads, and its rays cast a serenity and an inexpressible melancholy upon the fields and woods—it was a celestial eye, which opened upon this sleeping and lovely country.

From Rheims to Bethel there is nothing interesting, and the latter place affords little worthy of remark.

On arriving at Mezières I anxiously looked on all sides for the ruins of the ancient castle of Hellebarde, but could not perceive them. The church of Mezières is of the fifteenth century, and has, to the right and left of the choir, two *bas-reliefs* of the time of Charles the Eighth. On the north of the *apside* I perceived an inscription upon the wall, which testified that Mezières was cruelly assailed and bombarded by the Prussians in 1815; and above it these words:—

" *Lector leva oculos ad fornicem et vide quasi quoddam divinæ manus indicium.*"

I raised my eyes and saw a large rent in the

vault above my head, and in it an enormous bomb, which, after having pierced the roof of the church, the timber-work, and the masonry, was thus stopped, as if by miracle, when about to fall upon the pavement. Twenty-five years have now expired, and still it remains in the same position. That bomb, and that wide rent which is above the head of the visitor, produce a very strange effect, which is heightened upon reflecting that the first bomb made use of in war was at Mezières, in the year 1521. On the other side of the church another inscription informs us that the nuptials of Charles the Ninth with Elizabeth of Austria were happily celebrated in this church, on the 17th November, 1570, two years before St. Bartholomew. The grand *portail* is of this epoch, and, consequently, noble in appearance, and of a refined taste.

As for Mezières—there are some very tall trees upon its ramparts: the streets are clean, and remarkable for their dullness; there is nothing about the town that reminds us of Hellebarde and Garinus, the founders; Balthazar, who ransacked it; Count Hugo, who ennobled it; or of Folques and Adalberon, who besieged it.

It was near noon when I arrived at Sédan, and, instead of seeing monuments and edifices, I saw what the town contains—pretty women, handsome *carabiniers*, cannons, and trees and prairies

along the Meuse. I tried to find some vestiges
of M. de Turenne, but did not succeed. The
pavilion where he was born is demolished, but a
black stone, with the following inscription, sup-
plies its place :

> " ICI NAQUIT TURENNE
> LE II SEPTEMBRE MDCXI."

The date, which is in prominent gold letters,
struck me, and my mind reverted to that event-
ful period. In 1611 Sully retired ; Henry the
Fourth was assassinated the preceding year ;
Louis the Thirteenth, who ought to have died
as his father did, on the 14th of May, was
then ten years old ; Richelieu was in his twenty-
sixth year ; the good people of Rouen called a
man *Petit Pierre*, who was afterwards named
by the universe *le Grand Corneille ;* Shakspeare
and Cervantes were living, so were Branthome
and Pierre Mathieu. In 1611 Papirien Masson and
Jean Bussée breathed their last ; Gustave Adolphe
succeeded the visionary monarch Charles the
Ninth of Sweden ; Philip the Third, in spite of
the advice of the Duke of Osunna, drove the
Moors from Spain ; and the German astronomer,
Jean Fabricius, discovered the spots on the sun.
Such are the events that were transpiring in
the world when Turenne was born. Sédan has
not been a pious guardian of his memory, nor, in
fact, has it in its annals any *souvenirs* of William

de la March, the Boar of Ardennes, the frightful predecessor of Turenne.

After having made a good breakfast in the Hotel de la Croix d'Or, I decided on returning on foot to Mezières, and to take the coach for Givet. The distance is five leagues, but the road is truly picturesque, running along the valley of the Meuse. About a league from Sédan we meet Douchery, with its old wooden bridge and fine trees; villages, with smiling urchins, chatelets, shrouded in massive verdure, where sheep and oxen are grazing in the sun.

I arrived at Mezières at seven in the evening, and at eight, seated in a miserable *coupé*, between a *Sir John Falstaff* and a female who might well have passed for his better half, set out for Givet. The two *gros etres* began to converse, and spoke of events as striking as they were stirring—such as, " that it is now twenty-two years since I was at Rocroy,"—"that M. Crochard, the secretary of the under-prefecture, is his intimate friend,"— " that, as it is twelve at night, the good Mons. Crochard must be in bed."

Day dawned. We approached a drawbridge, which was lowered, and shortly afterwards we entered into a narrow street, that led into a court, where servants came running with candles in their hands, and grooms with lanterns. I was at Givet.

CHAPTER V.

GIVET.

Flemish Architects. — Little Givet. — The Inscription. — Jose
Gutierez.—The Peasant Girl.

THIS is an exceedingly pretty town, situated on the Meuse, which separates Great
from Little Givet, and is headed by a ridge of
rocks, at the summit of which is the fort of
Charlemont. The *auberge*, called the Hotel of
the Golden Mount, is very comfortable; and
travelers may find refreshments there, which,
though not the most exquisite, are palatable to
the hungry, and a bed, though not the softest in
the world, highly acceptable to the weary.

The steeple of Little Givet is of simple construction; that of Great Givet is more complicated—more *recherché*. The worthy architect, in
planning the latter, had, without doubt, recourse
to the following mode : — He took a priest's
square cap, on which he placed bottom upwards,
a large plate; above this plate a sugar-loaf
headed with a bottle, a steel spike thrust into its
neck; and on the spike he perched a cock, the
purport of which was to inform its beholders the
way that the wind blew. Supposing that he took

a day to each idea, he therefore must have rested the seventh. This artist was certainly Flemish.

About two centuries ago Flemish architects imagined that nothing could exceed in beauty gigantic pieces of slate, resembling kitchen-ware, —so, when they had a steeple to build, they profited by the occasion, and decked their towns with a host of colossal plates.

Nevertheless, a view of Givet still has charms, especially if taken towards evening from the middle of the bridge. When I viewed it, night, which helps to screen the foolish acts of man, had begun to cast its mantle over the *contour* of this singularly-built steeple; smoke was hovering about the roofs of the houses; at my left, the elms were softly rustling; to my right, an ancient tower was reflected on the bosom of the Meuse; further on, at the foot of the redoubtable rock of Charlemont, I descried, like a white line, a long edifice, which I found to be nothing more than an uninhabited country house; above the town, the towers, and steeples, an immense ridge of rocks hid the horizon from my sight; and in the distance, in a clear sky, the half-moon appeared with so much purity—with so much of heaven in it—that I imagined that God had exposed to our view part of his nuptial ring to testify his wedded affection to man.

Next day I determined to visit the venerable

turret which crowned, in seeming respect, little
Givet. The road is steep, and commands the
services of both hands and feet. After some in-
considerable trouble, and no slight labor of all-
fours, I reached the foot of the tower, which is
fast falling into ruin, where I found a huge door
secured by a large padlock. I knocked and
shouted, but no one answered, so I was obliged
to descend without gratifying my curiosity. My
pains, however, were not altogether lost, for, on
passing the old edifice, I discovered among the
rubbish, which is daily crumbling into dust and
falling into the stream, a large stone, on which
were the vestiges of an inscription. I examined
them attentively, but could only make out the
following letters:

> " LOQVE . . . SA . L . OMBRE
> PARAS . . . MODI . SL .
> ACAV . P . . . SOTROS."

Above these letters, which seem to have been
scratched with a nail, the signature, " IOSE
GVITEREZ, 1643," remained entire.

Inscriptions, from boyhood, always interested
me; and I assure you, this one opened up a vein
of thought and inquiry. What did this inscription signify?—in what language was it written?
By making some allowance for orthography, one
might imagine that it was French; but, on con-
sidering that the words *para* and *otros* were

Spanish, I concluded that it must have been written in Castilian. After some reflection, I imagined that these were the original words :—

> " LO QUE EMPESA EL HOMBRE
> PARA SIMISMO DIOS LE
> ACAVA PARA LOS OTROS."

—"What man begins for himself, God finishes for others."

But who was this Gutierez? The stone had evidently been taken from the interior of the tower. It was in 1643 that the battle of Rocroy was fought. Was Jose Gutierez, then, one of the vanquished? had he, to while away the long and tiresome days, written on the walls of the dungeon, the melancholy *résumé* of his life, and of that of all mankind—

> " *Ce que l'homme commence pour lui, Dieu l'achève pour les autres ?* "

At five o'clock next morning, alone, and comfortably seated on the *banquette* of the diligence Van Gend, I left *la France* by the route of Namur. We proceeded by the only chain of mountains of which Belgium can boast; for the Meuse, by continuing to flow in opposition to the *abaissement* of the *plateau* of Ardennes, succeeded in forming a plain which is now called Flanders—a plain to which nature has refused mountains for its protection, but which man has studded with fortresses.

After an ascension of half an hour, the horses became fatigued, the *conducteur* thirsty, and they (I might say we), with one accord stopped before a small wine-shop, in a poor but picturesque village, built on the two sides of a ravine cut through the mountains. This ravine, which is at one time the bed of a torrent, and at another the leading street of the village, is paved with the granite of the surrounding mountains. When we were passing, six harnessed horses proceeded, or rather climbed, along that strange and frightfully steep street, drawing after them a large empty vehicle with four wheels. If it had been laden, I am pursuaded that it would have required twenty horses to have drawn it. I can in no way account for the use of such carriages in this ravine, if they are not meant to serve as sketches for young Dutch painters, whom we met here and there upon the road—a bag upon their back, and a stick in their hand.

What can a person do on the outside of a coach but gaze at all that comes within his view? I could not be better situated for such a purpose. Before me was the greater portion of the valley of the Meuse ; to the south were the two Givets, graciously linked by their bridge ; to the west was the tower of Egmont, half in ruins, which was casting behind it an immense shadow ; to the north were the sombre trenches into which the

3

Meuse was emptying itself, whence a light blue
vapor arose. On turning my head, my eyes fell
upon a handsome peasant-girl, who was sitting
by the open window of a cottage, dressing herself; and above the hut of the *paysanne*, but
almost close to view, were the formidable bat-
teries of Charlemont, which crowned the frontiers
of France.

Whilst I was contemplating this *coup dœil*, the
peasant-girl lifted her eyes, and on perceiving
me, she smiled; saluted me graciously; then,
without shutting the window or appearing disconcerted. she continued her toilette.

CHAPTER VI.

THE BANKS OF THE MEUSE—DINANT—NAMUR.

The Lesse.—A Flemish Garden.—The Mannequin.—The Tombstone.—Athletic Demoiselles.—Signboards and their utility.

I HAVE arrived at Liege. The route from
Givet, following the course of the Meuse, is
highly picturesque; and it strikes me as singular
that so little has been said of the banks of this
river, for they are truly beautiful and romantic.

After passing the cabin of the peasant-girl, the
road is full of windings, and during a walk of
three-quarters of an hour we are in a thick forest,
interspersed with ravines and torrents. Then
a long plain intervenes, at the extremity of
which is a frightful yawning—a tremendous
precipice, upwards of three hundred feet in
depth. At the foot of the precipice, amidst
the brambles which bordered it, the Meuse
is seen meandering peacefully, and on its
banks is a *chatelet* resembling a *patisserie mani-
érée,* or time-piece, of the days of Louis the
Fifteenth, with its decorated walls, and its Lilliputian and fantastical garden. Nothing is more
singularly striking and more ridiculous than this
—the petty work of man, surrounded by Nature
in all her sublimity. One is apt to say that it is a

shocking demonstration of the bad taste of man,
brought into contrast with the sublime poetry of
God.

After the gulf, the plain begins again, for the
ravine of the Meuse divides it as the rut of a
wheel cuts the ground.

About a quarter of a league further on, the
road becomes very steep, and leads abruptly to
the river. The declivity here is charming.
Vine-branches encircle the hawthorn, which
crowd both sides of the road. The Meuse at
this point is straight, green in appearance, and
runs to the left between two banks thickly
studded with trees. A bridge is next seen, then
another river, smaller yet equally beautiful,
which empties itself into the Meuse. It is the
Lesse; three leagues from which, in a cavity on
the right, is the famed grotto of Hansur Lesse.

On turning the road, a huge pyramidal rock,
sharpened like the spire of a cathedral, suddenly
appears. The *conducteur* told me that it was the
Roche à Bazard. The road passes between the
mountain and this colossal *borne*, then turns
again, and at the foot of an enormous block of
granite, crowned with a citadel, a church, and a
long street of old houses meet the eye. It is
Dinant.

We stopped here about a quarter of an hour,
and observed a little garden in the diligence-

yard, which is sufficient to warn the traveler that he is in Flanders. The flowers in it are very pretty: in the midst are two painted statues, the one represents a woman, or rather a mannequin, for it is clothed in an Indian gown, with an old silk bonnet. On approaching, an indistinct noise strikes the ear and a strange spurting of water is perceived. We then discovered that this female is a fountain.

After leaving Dinant, the valley extends, and the Meuse gradually widens. On the right hand of the river, the ruins of two ancient castles present themselves; the rocks are now only to be seen here and there under a rich covering of verdure; and a *housse* of green *velours*, bordered with flowers, covers the face of the country.

On this side are hop-fields, orchards, and trees burdened with fruit; on that, the laden vine is ever appearing, amongst whose leaves the feathery tribe are joyously reveling. Here the cackling of ducks is heard, there the chuckling of hens. Young girls, their arms naked to the shoulder, are seen jocosely walking along, with laden baskets on their heads; and from time to time a village churchyard meets the eye, contrasting strangely with the neighboring road—so full of joy, of beauty, and of life.

In one of those churchyards, whose dilapidated walls leave exposed to view tall grass, green and

blooming, mocking, as it were, the once vain
mortal that moulders beneath, I read on a tombstone the following inscription—

"O PIE, DEFUNCTIS MISERIS SUCCURRE, VIATOR?"

No *memento* had ever such an effect upon me
as this one. Ordinarily, the dead warn—there,
they supplicate.

After passing a hill, where the rocks, sculptured by the rain, resembled the half-worn and
blackened stones of the old fountain of Luxembourg, we begin to perceive our approximation
to Namur. Gentlemen's country seats begin to
mix with the abodes of peasants, and the villa is
no sooner passed than we come to a village.

The diligence stopped at one of these places,
where I had, on one side, a garden well ornamented with colonnades and Ionic temples; on
the other, a *cabaret*, at the door of which a number of men and women were drinking; and to
the right, upon a pedestal of white marble,
veined by the shadows of the branches, a Venus
de Medicis, half hid among leaves, as if ashamed
to be seen in her nudid state by a group of
peasants.

A few steps further on, were two or three
good-looking, athletic wenches, perched upon a
plum-tree of considerable height; one of them
in a rather *delicate* attitude, but perfectly re-

gardless of and unregarded by the peasants underneath.

About an hour afterwards we arrived at Namur, which is situated near the junction of the Sombre and the Meuse. The women are pretty, and the men are handsome, and they have something pleasing and affable in their cast of countenance. As to the town itself, there is nothing remarkable in it; nor has it anything in its general appearance which speaks of its antiquity. There are no monuments, no architecture, no edifices worthy of notice; in fact, Namur can boast of nothing but mean-looking churches and fountains, of the *mauvais gout* of Louis XV. The town is crowned, gloomily and sadly, by the citadel. However, I must say that I looked upon these fortifications with a feeling of respect, for they had once the honor of being attacked by Vauban and defended by Cohorn.

CHAPTER VII.

THE BANKS OF THE MEUSE—HUY—LIEGE.

A Chapel of the Tenth Century.—Iron Works of Mr. Cockerill ; their singular appearance.—St. Paul's at Liege.—Palace of the Ecclesiastical Princes of Liege.—Significant decorations of a room at Liege.

ON leaving Namur we entered a magnificent avenue of trees, whose foliage serves to hide from our view the town, with its mean and uncouth steeples, which, seen at a distance, have a grotesque and singular appearance. After passing those fine trees, the fresh breeze from the Meuse reaches us, and the road begins to wend cheerfully along the river side. The Meuse widens by the junction of the Sombre, the valley extends, and the double walls of rocks reappear, resembling now and then, Cyclop fortresses, great dungeons in ruins, and vast *Titaniques* towers.

The rocks of the Meuse contain a great quantity of iron. When viewed in the landscape, they are of a beautiful color ; but broken, they change into that odious greyish-blue which pervades all Belgium. That which is magnificent in mountains loses the grandeur, when broken and converted into houses

"It is God who forms the rocks; man is the builder of habitations."

We passed hastily through a little village called Sanson, near which stand the ruins of a castle, built, it is said, in the days of Clodion. The rocks at this place represent the face of a man, to which the *conducteur* never fails to direct the attention of the traveler. We then came to the Ardennes, where I observed—what would be highly appreciated by antiquaries—a little rustic church, still entire, of the tenth century. In another village (I think it is Sclayen) is seen the following inscription, in large characters, above the principal door of the church:—

"LES CHIENS HORS DE LA MAISON DE DIEU."

If I were the worthy curate, I should deem it more important for men to enter, than dogs to go out.

After passing the Ardennes, the mountains become scattered, and the Meuse, no longer running by the roadside, crosses among prairies. The country is still beautiful, but the *cheminée de l'usine*—that sad obelisk of our *civilisation industrielle*—too often strikes the eye. The road again joins the river: we perceive vast fortifications, like eagles' nests, perched upon rocks; a fine church of the fourteenth century; and an old bridge with seven arches. We are at Huy.

3*

Huy and Dinant are the prettiest towns upon
the Meuse; the former about half way between
Namur and Liege, the latter half way between
Namur and Givet. Huy, which is at present a
redoubtable citadel, was in former times a warlike
commune, and held out with valor a siege with
Liege, as Dinant did with Namur. In those
heroic times, cities, as kingdoms now, were
always declaring war against each other.

After leaving Huy, we from time to time see
on the banks of the river a zinc manufactory,
which, from its blackened aspect with smoke escaping through the creviced roofs, appears to us
as if a fire were breaking out, or like a house
after a fire has been nearly extinguished. By the
side of a bean field, in the perfume of a little
garden, a brick house with a slate turret, the vine
clinging to its walls, doves on the roof, and cages
at the windows, strikes the eye—we then think
of Teniers and Mieris.

The shades of evening approached—the wind
ceased blowing, the trees rustling—and nothing
was heard but the rippling of the water. The
lights in the adjacent houses burnt dimly, and all
objects were becoming obscured. The passengers yawned, and said, "We shall be at Liege in
an hour." At this moment a singular sight suddenly presented itself. At the foot of the hills,
which were scarcely perceptible, two round balls

of fire glared like the eyes of tigers. By the
roadside was a frightful dark chimney stalk, surmounted by a huge flame, which cast a sombre
hue upon the adjoining rocks, forests, and ravines.
Nearer the entry of the valley, hidden in the
shade, was a mouth of live coal, which suddenly
opened and shut, and, in the midst of frightful
noises, spouted forth a tongue of fire. It was the
lighting of the furnaces.

After passing the place called Little Flemalle,
the sight was inexpressible—was truly magnificent. All the valley seemed to be in a state of
conflagration—smoke issuing from this place, and
flames arising from that; in fact, we could imagine that a hostile army had ransacked the
country, and that twenty districts presented, in
that night of darkness, all the aspects and phases
of a conflagration—some catching fire, some enveloped in smoke, and others surrounded with
flames.

This aspect of war is caused by peace—this
frightful symbol of devastation is the effect of
industry. The furnaces of the iron works of Mr.
Cockerill, where cannon is cast of the largest
calibre, and steam engines of the highest power
are made, alone meet the eye.

A wild and violent noise comes from this chaos
of industry. I had the curiosity to approach one
of these frightful places, and I could not help

admiring the assiduity of the workmen. It was a prodigious spectacle, to which the solemnity of the hour lent a supernatural aspect. Wheels, saws, boilers, cylinders, scales—all those monstrous implements that are called machines, and to which steam gives a frightful and noisy life— rattle, grind, shriek, hiss; and at times, when the blackened workmen thrust the hot iron into the water, a moaning sound is heard like that of hydras and dragons tormented in hell by demons.

———

Liege is one of those old towns which are in a fair way of becoming new—deplorable transformation! one of those towns where things of antiquity are disappearing, leaving in their places white facades, enriched with painted statues; where the good old buildings, with slated roofs, skylight windows, chiming bells, belfries, and weathercocks, are falling into decay, while gazed at with horror by some thick-headed citizen, who is busy with a *Constitutionnel*, reading what he does not understand, yet pompous with the supposed knowledge which he has attained. The *Octroi*, a Greek temple, represents a castle flanked with towers, and thick set with pikes; and the long stalks of the furnaces supply the place of the elegant steeples of the churches. The an-

cient city was, perhaps, noisy ; the modern one
is productive of smoke.

Liege has no longer the enormous cathedral of
the *princeséveques,* built by the illustrious Bishop
Notger in the year 1000, and demolished in 1795
by—no one can tell whom ; but it can boast of
the iron works of Mr. Cockerill.

Neither has it any longer the convent of Do-
minicans—sombre cloister of high fame ! noble
edifice of fine architecture ! but there is a theater
exactly on the same spot, decorated with pillars
and brass capitals, where operas are performed.

Liege, in the nineteenth century, is what it was
in the sixteenth.   It vies with France in implements of war; with Versailles, in extravagance
of arms.   But the old city of Saint Hubert, with
its church and fortress, its ecclesiastical and military *commune,* has ceased to be a city of prayer
and of war; it is one of buying and selling—an
immense hive of industry.   It has been transformed into a rich commercial center ; and has
put one of its arms in France, the other in Holland, and is incessantly taking from the one and
receiving from the other.

Everything has been changed in this city ;
even its etymology has not escaped.   The ancient
stream Legia bears now the appellation of Ri-
de-Coq Fontaine.

Notwithstanding, we must admit that Liege is

advantageously situated near the green brow of the mountain of Sainte Walburge; is divided by the Meuse into the lower and upper towns; is interspersed with thirteen bridges, some of which have rather an architectural appearance; and is surrounded with trees, hills, and prairies. It has turrets, clocks, and *portes-donjons*, like that of Saint Martin and Amerrcœur, to excite the poet or the antiquary, even though he be startled with the noise, the smoke, and the flames of the manufactories around.

As it rained heavily, I only visited four churches:—Saint Paul's, the *actuelle* cathedral, is a noble building of the fifteenth century, having a Gothic cloister, with a charming *portail* of the Renaissance, and surmounted by a belfry, which, had it not been that some inapt architect of our day spoiled all the angles, would be considered elegant. Saint Jean is a grave façade of the sixteenth century, consisting of a large square steeple, with a smaller one on each side. Saint Hubert is rather a superior-looking building, whose lower galleries are of an excellent *ordre*. Saint Denis, a curious church of the tenth century, with a large steeple of the eleventh. That steeple bears traces of having been injured by fire. It was probably burnt during the Norman outbreak. The Roman architecture has been ingeniously repaired, and the

steeple finished in brick. This is perfectly dis-
cernible, and has a most singular effect.

As I was going from Saint Denis to Saint
Hubert by a labyrinth of old narrow streets,
ornamented here and there with *madones*, I suddenly came within view of a large dark stone
wall, and on close observation discovered that
the back facade indicated that it was a palace of
the middle age. An obscure door presented itself; I entered, and at the expiration of a few
moments found myself in a vast yard, which
turned out to be that of the palace of the Ecclesiastic Princes of Liege. The *ensemble* of the
architecture is, perhaps, the most gloomy and
noble-looking that I ever saw.

There are four lofty granite facades, surmounted by four prodigious slate roofs, with the
same number of galleries. Two of the facades,
which are perfectly entire, present the admirable
adjustment of ogives and arches which characterized the end of the fifteenth century and the
beginning of the sixteenth. The windows of
this clerical palace have *meneaux* like those of a
church. Unfortunately the two other facades,
which were destroyed by fire in 1734, have been
rebuilt in the pitiful style of that epoch, and tend
to detract from the general effect. It is now 105
years since the last bishop occupied this fine
structure.

The quadruple gallery that walls the yard is admirably preserved. There is nothing more pleasing to study than the pillars upon which the ogives are placed : they are of gray granite, like the rest of the palace. Whilst examining the four rows, one half of the shaft of the pillar disappears, sometimes at the top, then at the bottom, under a rich swelling of *arabesques*. The swelling is doubled in the west range of the pillars, and the stalk disappears entirely. This speaks only of the Flemish caprice of the sixteenth century ; but what perplexes us is, that the chapiters of these pillars, decorated with heads, foliage, apocalyptical figures, dragons, and hieroglyphics, seem to belong to the architecture of the eleventh century ; and it must be remembered that the palace of Liege was commenced in 1508, by Prince Erard de la Mark, who reigned thirty-two years.

This grave edifice is at present a court of justice ; booksellers, and toy-merchants' shops are under all the arches, and vegetable stalls in the courtyard. The black robes of the law practitioners are seen in the midst of baskets of red and green cabbages. Groups of Flemish merchants, some merry, others morose, make fun and quarrel before each pillar ; irritated pleaders appear from all the windows ; and in that sombre yard, formerly solitary and tranquil as a convent, of which it has the appearance, the untired tongue of the advocate mingles with the chatter, the noise, and *bavardage* of the buyers and sellers.

My room at Liege was ornamented with muslin curtains, upon which were embroidered—not nosegays, but melons. There were also several pictures, representing the triumph of the Allies and our disasters in 1814. Behold the *legende* printed at the bottom of one of these paintings:—

"Battle of Arcis-sur-Aube, 21st March, 1814 The greater portion of the garrison of this place composed of the *garde ancienne*, were taken prisoners, and the Allies, on the 22nd of April, triumphantly entered Paris."

CHAPTER VIII.

THE BANKS OF THE VESDRE.—VERVIERS.

Railways.—Miners at Work.—Louis the Fourteenth.

YESTERDAY morning, as the diligence was about to leave Liege for Aix-la-Chapelle, a *worthy* citizen annoyed the passengers by refusing to take the seat upon the *imperiale* which the conductor pointed out as his. For the sake of peace I offered him mine ; which the condescending traveler, without evincing any reluctance, or even thanking me, accepted, and the heavy vehicle forthwith rolled tardily along. I was pleased with the change. The road, though no longer by the banks of the Meuse, but by those of the Vesdre, is exceedingly beautiful.

The Vesdre is rapid, and runs through Verviers and Chauffontaines, along the most charming valley in the world. In August, especially if the day be fine, with a blue sky over head, we have either a ravine or a garden, and certainly always a paradise. From the road the river is ever in sight. It at one time passes through a pleasing village, at another it skirts an old castle with square turrets ; there the country suddenly changes its aspect, and, on turning by a hillside, the eye discovers, through an opening in a thick tuft of trees, a low house, with a huge wheel by its side. It is a water-mill.

Between Chauffontaines and Verviers the valley is full of charms, and, the weather being propitious, added much to enliven the scene. Marmosets were playing upon the garden steps ; the breeze was shaking the leaves of the tall poplars, and sounded like the music of peace, the harmony of nature ; handsome heifers, in groups of three and four, were reposing on the greensward, shaded by leafy blinds from the rays of the sun ; then, far from all houses, and alone, a fine cow, worthy of the regard of Argus, was peacefully grazing. The soft notes of a flute floating on the breeze were distinctly heard.

" Mercurius septem mulcet arundinibus."

The railway—that *colossale entreprise*, which runs from Anvers to Liege, and is being extended to Verviers — is cut through the solid rock, and runs along the valley. Here we meet a bridge, there a viaduct ; and at times we see in the distance, at the foot of an immense rock, a group of dark objects, resembling a hillock of ants, busily blasting the solid granite.

These ants, small though they be, perform the work of giants.

When the fissure is wide and deep, a strange sound proceeds from the interior; in fact, one might imagine that the rock is making known its grievances by the mouth which man has made.

Verviers is an insignificant little town, divided into three *quartiers*, called Chick-Chack, Brasse-Crotte, and Dardanelle. In passing, I observed a little urchin, about six years of age, who, seated on a door-step, was smoking his pipe, with all the magisterial air of a Grand Turk. The *marmot fumier* looked into my face, and burst into a fit of laughter, which made me conclude that my appearance was to him rather ridiculous.

After Verviers, the road skirts the Vesdre as far as Simbourg: Simbourg—that town of counts, that *paté* which Louis the Fourteenth found had *a crust rather hard for mastication*—is at present a dismantled fortress.

CHAPTER IX.

AIX-LA-CHAPELLE—THE TOMB OF CHARLEMAGNE.

Legend of the Wolf and Pine-Apple.—Carlo-Magno.—Barber·
ousse. — The Untombing of Charlemagne. — Exhibition of
Relics. — Arm-chair of Charlemage. — The Swiss Guide. —
Hotel-de-Ville, the Birthplace of Charlemagne.

FOR an invalid, Aix-la-Chapelle is a mineral
fountain—warm, cold, irony, and sulphur-
ous ; for the tourist, it is a place for redoubts and
concerts ; for the pilgrim, the place of relics,
where the gown of the Virgin Mary, the blood
of Jesus, the cloth which enveloped the head of
John the Baptist after his decapitation, are exhibited every seven years ; for the antiquarian, it
is a noble abbey of *filles à abbesse*, connected
with the male convent, which was built by Saint
Gregory, son of Nicephore, Emperor of the East ;
for the hunter, it is the ancient valley of the
wild boars ; for the merchant, it is a *fabrique* of
cloth, needles, and pins ; and for him who is no
merchant, manufacturer, hunter, antiquary, pilgrim, tourist, or invalid, it is the city of Charlemagne.

Charlemagne was born at Aix-la-Chapelle, and
died there. He was born in the old place, of
which there now only remains the tower, and he

was buried in the church that he founded in 796, two years after the death of his wife Frastrada. Leon the Third consecrated it in 804, and tradition says that two bishops of Tongres, who were buried at Maestricht, arose from their graves, in order to complete, at that ceremony, 365 bishops and archbishops—representing the days of the year.

This historical and legendary church, from which the town has taken its name, has undergone, during the last thousand years, many transformations.

No sooner had I entered Aix than I went to the chapel.

The *portail*, built of grey-blue granite, is of the time of Louis the Fifteenth, with doors of the eighth century. To the right of the *portail*, a large bronze ball, like a pine-apple, is placed upon a granite pillar; and on the opposite side, on another pillar, is a wolf, of the same metal, which is half turned towards the bystanders, its mouth half open and its teeth displayed. This is the legend of the wolf and pine-apple, daily recited by the old women of the place to the inquiring traveler:—

"A long time ago, the good people of Aix-la-Chapelle wished to build a church: money was put aside for the purpose; the foundation was laid, the walls were built, and the timber work was commenced. For six months there was nothing heard but a deafening noise of saws, hammers, and axes; but at the expiration of that period the money ran short. A call was made upon the pilgrims for assistance, and a plate was placed at the door of the church, but scarcely a liard was collected. What was to be done? The senate assembled, and proposed, argued, advised, and consulted. The workmen refused to continue their labor. The grass, the brambles, the ivy, and all the other insolent weeds which surround ruins, clang to the new stones of the abandoned edifice. Was there no other alternative than that of discontinuing the church? The glorious senate of burgomasters were in a state of consternation.

"One day, in the midst of their discussions, a strange man, of tall stature and respectable appearance, entered.

"'Good day, gentlemen. What is the subject of discussion? You seem bewildered. Ah, I suppose your church weighs heavy at your hearts. You do not know how to finish it. People say that money is the chief requisite for its completion.'

"'Stranger,' said one of the senate, '*allez vous en au diable?* It would take a million of money.'

"'There is a million,' said the unknown, opening the window, and pointing to a chariot drawn by oxen, and guarded by twenty negroes armed to the teeth.

"One of the burgomasters went with the stranger to the carriage, took the first sack that came to his hand, then both returned. It was laid before the senate, and found to be full of gold.

"The *bourgomestres* looked with eyes expressive both of foolishness and surprise, and demanded of the stranger who he was.

"'My dear fellows, I am the man who has money at command. What more do you require? I inhabit the Black Forest, near the lake of Wildsée, and not far from the ruins of Heidenstadt, the city of Pagans. I possess mines of gold and silver, and at night I handle millions of precious stones. But I have strange fancies—in fact, I am unhappy, a melancholy being, passing my days in gazing into the transparent lake, watching the *tourniqnet* and the water tritons, and observing the growth of the *polygonum amphibium* among the rocks. But a truce to questions and idle stories. I have opened my heart —profit by it! There is your million of money. Will you accept it?'

"'*Pardieu, oui*,' said the senate. 'We shall finish our church.'

"'Well, it is yours,' the stranger said; 'but remember, there is a condition.'

" 'What is it?'

" ' Finish your church, gentlemen—take all this precious metal; but promise me, in exchange, the first soul that enters into the church on the day of its consecration.'

" ' You are the devil!' cried the senate.

" ' *You are imbeciles,*' replied Urian.

" The burgomasters began to cross themselves, to turn pale, and tremble; but Urian, who was a queer fellow, shook the bag containing the gold, laughed till he almost split his sides, and, soon gaining the confidence of the worthy gentlemen, a negotiation took place. The devil is a clever fellow—that is the reason that he is a devil.

" 'After all," he said, " I am the one who shall lose by the bargain. You shall have your million and your church: as for me, I shall only have a soul.'

" ' Whose soul, Sir?' demanded the frightened senate.

" ' The first that comes—that, perhaps, of some canting hypocrite, who to appear devout, and to show his zeal in the cause, will enter first. But, my friends, your church promises well. The plan pleases me; and the edifice, in my opinion, will be superb. I see with pleasure that your architect prefers the *trompe-sous-le-coin* to that of Montpellier. I do not dislike the arched vault, but still I would have preferred a ridged one. I

acknowledge that he has made the doorway very
tastefully : but I am not sure if he has been care-
ful about the thickness of the *parpain*. What is
the name of your architect? Tell him from me,
that, to make a door well, there must be four
panels. Nevertheless, the church is of a very
good style, and well adjusted. It would be a pity
to leave off what has been so well begun. You
must finish your church. Come, my friends; the
million for you—the soul for me. Is it not so?'

" ' After all,' thought the citizens, ' we ought
to be satisfied that he contents himself with one
soul. He might, if he observed attentively, find
that there is scarcely one in the whole place that
does not belong to him.'

" The bargain was concluded—the million was
locked up—Urian disappeared in a blue flame—
and two years afterwards the church was finished.

" You must know that all the senators took an
oath to keep the transaction a profound secret ;
and it must also be understood that each of them
on the very same evening related the affair to
his wife. When the church was complete, the
whole town—thanks to the wives of the senators
—knew the secret of the senate; and no one
would enter the church. This was an embarrassment greater even than the first: the church was
erected. but no one would enter: it was finished.

but it was empty. What good was a church of
this description?

"The senate assembled, but they could do
nothing; and they called upon the Bishop of
Tongres, but he was equally puzzled. The
canons of the church were consulted; but to no
avail. At last the monks were brought in.

" ' *Pardieu !* ' said one of them; 'you seem to
stand on trifles; you owe Urian the first soul
that passes the door of the church; but he did
not stipulate as to the kind of soul. I assure
you this Urian is at the best an ass. Gentlemen, after a severe struggle, a wolf was taken
alive in the valley of Borcette. Make it enter
the church. Urian must be contented; he shall
have a soul, although only that of a wolf.'

" ' Bravo! bravo!' shouted the senate.

"At the dawn of the following day the bells
rang.

" ' What!' cried the inhabitants—'to-day is
the consecration of the church, but who will dare
to enter first?'

" I won't!' shouted one. ' Nor I !'—' Nor I !'
escaped from the lips of the others.

"At last the senate and the *chapitre* arrived,
followed by men carrying the wolf in a cage. A
signal was given to open the door of the church
and that of the cage simultaneously; the wolf,
half mad from fright, rushed into the empty

church, where Urian was waiting, his mouth open, and his eyes shut. Judge of his rage when he discovered that he had swallowed a wolf. He shouted tremendously, flew for some time under the high arches, making a noise like a tempest, and, on going out, gave the door a furious kick, and rent it from top to bottom."

It is upon that account, say the old dames, that a statue of the wolf has been placed on the left side of the church, and an apple, which represents its poor soul, on the right.

I must add, before finishing the legend, that I looked for the rent made by the heel of the devil, but could not find it.

On approaching the chapel of the great *portail* the effect is not striking; the facade displays the different styles of architecture—Roman, Gothic, and modern,—without order, and consequently, without grandeur; but if, on the contrary, we arrive at the chapel by Chevet, the result is otherwise. The high *abside* of the fourteenth century, in all its boldness and beauty, the rich workmanship of its balustrades, the variety of its *gargouilles*, the sombre hue of the stones, and the large, transparent windows—strike the beholder with admiration.

Here, nevertheless, the aspect of the church —imposing though it is—will be found far from uniform. Between the *abside* and the *portail*, in a kind of cavity, the dome of Otho III., built over the tomb of Charlemagne in the tenth century, is hid from view. After a few moments' contemplation, a singular awe comes over us when gazing at this extraordinary edifice—an edifice which, like the great work that Charlemagne began, remains unfinished; and which, like his empire that spoke all languages, is composed of architecture that represents all styles. To the reflective, there is a strange analogy between that wonderful man and this great building.

After having passed the arched roof of the portico, and left behind me the antique bronze doors surmounted with lions' heads, a white rotundo of two stories, in which all the *fantaisies* of architecture are displayed, attracted my attention. At casting my eyes upon the ground, I perceived a large block of black marble, with the following inscription in brass letters:—

"CAROLO MAGNO."

Nothing is more contemptible than to see, exposed to view, the bastard graces that surround this great Carlovingian name; angels resembling distorted Cupids, palm-branches like colored feathers, garlands of flowers, and knots of ribbons, are placed under the dome of Otho III., and upon the tomb of Charlemagne.

The only thing here that evinces respect to the shade of that great man is an immense lamp, twelve feet in diameter, with forty-eight burners; which was presented, in the twelfth century, by Barberousse. It is of brass, gilt with gold, has the form of a crown, and is suspended from the ceiling above the marble stone by an iron chain about seventy feet in length.

It is evident that some other monument had been erected to Charlemagne. There is nothing to convince us that this marble, bordered with brass, is of antiquity. As to the letters, "CAROLO MAGNO," they are not of a later date than 1730.

Charlemagne is no longer under this stone. In 1166 Frederick Barberousse—whose gift, magnificent though it was, does by no means compensate for this sacrilege—caused the remains of that great emperor to be untombed. The Church claimed the imperial skeleton, and, separating the bones, made each a holy relic. In the adjoining sacristy, a vicar shows the people—for three francs seventy-five centimes—the fixed price— *the arm of Charlemagne*—that arm which held for a time the reins of the world. Venerable relic! which has the following inscription, written by some scribe of the twelfth century:

' Brachium Sancti Caroli Magni."

After that I saw the skull of Charlemagne,

that cranium which may be said to have been the mould of Europe, and which a beadle had the effrontery to strike with his finger.

All are kept in a wooden armory, with a few angels, similar to those I have just mentioned, on the top. Such is the tomb of the man whose memory has outlived ten ages, and who, by his greatness, has shed the rays of immortality around his name. *Sanctus, magnus,* belong to him—two of the most august epithets which this earth could bestow upon a human being.

There is one thing astonishing—that is, the largeness of the skull and arm. Charlemagne was, in fact, colossal with respect to size of body as well as extraordinary mental endowments. The son of Pepin-le-Bref was in body, as in mind, gigantic; of great corporeal strength, and of astounding intellect.

An inspection of this armory has a strange effect upon the antiquary. Besides the skull and arm, it contains the heart of Charlemagne; the cross which the emperor had round his neck in his tomb; a handsome *ostensoir,* of the Renaissance, given by Charles the Fifth, and spoiled, in the last century, by tasteless ornaments; fourteen richly sculptured gold plates, which once ornamented the arm-chair of the emperor; an *ostensoir,* given Philippe the Second; the cord which bound our Saviour; the sponge that was used upon the cross; the girdle of the Holy Virgin, and that of the Redeemer.

In the midst of innumerable ornaments, heaped up in the armory like mountains of gold and precious stones, are two shrines of singular beauty. One, the oldest, which is seldom opened, contains the remaining bones of Charlemagne, and the other, of the twelfth century, which Frederick Barberousse gave to the church, holds the relics, which are exhibited every seven years. A single exhibition of this shrine, in 1696, attracted 42,000 pilgrims, and drew, in ten days, 80,000 florins.

This shrine has only one key, which is in two pieces; the one is in the possession of the chapitre, the other in that of the magistrates of the town. Sometimes it is opened on extraordinary occasions, such as on the visit of a monarch.

In a small armory, adjoining the one mentioned, I saw an exact imitation of the Germanic crown of Charlemagne. That which he wore as Emperor of Germany is at Vienna; the one as King of France, at Rheims; and the other, as King of Lombardy, is at Menza, near Milan.

On going out of the sacristy, the beadle gave orders to one of the menials, a Swiss, to show me the interior of the chapel. The first object that fixed my attention was the pulpit, presented by

the Emperor Henry the Second, which is ex-
travagantly ornamented and gilt, in the style of
the eleventh century. To the right of the altar,
the heart of M. Antoine Berdolet, the first and
last Bishop of Aux-la-Chapelle, is encased. That
church had but one Bishop—he whom Buonaparte named "*Primus Aquisgranensis Episcopus.*"

In a dark room in the chapel, my conductor
opened another armory, which contained the sarcophagus of Charlemagne. It is a magnificent
coffin of white marble, upon which the carrying
off of Proserpine is sculptured. The fair girl is
represented as making desperate efforts to disen-
tangle herself from the grasp of Pluto, but the
god has seized her half-naked neck, and is forcing
her head against Minerva. Some of the nymphs,
the attendants of Proserpine, are in eager combat
with Furies, while others are endeavoring to
stop the car, which is drawn by two dragons. A
goddess has boldly seized one of them by the
wing, and the animal, to all appearance, is crying
hideously. This *bas-relief* is a poem, powerful
and startling—like the pictures of Pagan Rome,
and like some of those of Rubens.

The tomb, before it became the sarcophagus
of Charlemagne, was, it is said, that of Augustus.

After mounting a narrow staircase, my guide
conducted me to a gallery which is called the
Hochmunster. In this place is the arm-chair of

4*

Charlemagne. It is low, exceedingly wide, with a round back; is formed of four pieces of white marble, without ornaments or sculpture, and has for a seat an oak board, covered with a cushion of red velvet. There are six steps up to it, two of which are of granite, the others of marble. On this chair sat—a crown upon his head, a globe in one hand, a sceptre in the other, a sword by his side, the imperial mantle over his shoulders, the cross of Christ round his neck, and his feet in the sarcophagus of Augustus,—Carlo Magno in his tomb, in which attitude he remained for three hundred and fifty-two years—from 852 to 1166, when Frederick Barberousse, coveting the chair for his coronation, entered the tomb. Barberousse was an illustrious prince and a valiant soldier; and it must, therefore, have been a moment singularly strange when this crowned man stood before the crowned corpse of Charlemagne—the one in all the majesty of empire, the other in all the majesty of death. The soldier overcame the shades of greatness; the living became the despoliator of inanimate worth. The chapel claimed the skeleton, and Barberousse the marble chair, which afterwards became the throne where thirty-six emperors were crowned. Ferdinand the First was the last; Charles the Fifth preceded him. The German emperors are now crowned at Frankfort.

I remained spell-bound near this chair, so simple, yet so grand. I gazed upon the marble
steps, marked by the feet of those thirty-six
Cæsars who had here seen the bursting forth
of their illustriousness, and who, each in his
turn, had ceased to be of the living. Thoughts
started in my mind, recollections flashed across
my memory. When Frederick Barberousse was
old, he determined for the second or third time
to engage in the Holy War. One day he
reached the banks of the beautiful river Cyd-
nus, and, being warm, took a fancy to bathe.
The man who could profane the tomb of
Charlemagne might well forget Alexander. He
entered the river; the cold seized him. Alexander was young, and survived; Barberousse
was old, and lost his life.

It appears to me as probable, that, one day or
another, the pious thought will strike some saint,
king, or emperor, to take the remains of Charlemagne from the armory where the sacristans
have placed them—gathered all that still exists
of that great skeleton—and place them once
more in the arm-chair, the Carlovingian diadem
upon the skull, the globe of the empire on the
arm, and the imperial mantle over the bones.

This would be a magnificent sight for him who
dared to look at the apparition. What thoughts
would crowd upon his mind when beholding the

son of Pepin in his tomb—he, who equalled in greatness Augustus or Sesostris: he, who in fiction, is a knight-errant, like Roland—a magician, like Merlin; for religion, a saint, like Peter or Jerome; for philosophy, civilization personifies him, and every thousand years assumes a giant form to traverse some profound abyss—civil wars, barbarism, revolutions; which calls himself at one time Cæsar, then Charlemagne, and at another time Napoleon.

In 1804, when Buonaparte became known as Napoleon, he visited Aix-la-Chapelle. Josephine, who accompanied him, had the caprice to sit down on this chair; but Napoleon, out of respect for Charlemagne, took off his hat, and remained for some time standing, and in silence. The following fact is somewhat remarkable, and struck me forcibly:— In 814 Charlemagne died; a thousand years afterwards, most probably about the same hour, Napoleon fell.

In that fatal year, 1814, the allied sovereigns visited the tomb of the great *Carolo.* Alexander of Russia, like Napoleon, took off his hat and uniform; Frederick William of Prussia kept on his *casquette de petite tenue;* Francis retained his surtout and round bonnet. The King of Prussia stood upon the marble steps, receiving information from the prévot of the chapitre respecting the coronation of the emperors of Germany;

the two emperors remained silent. Napoleon, Josephine, Alexander, Frederick William, and Francis, are now no more.

My guide, who gave me these details, was an old French soldier. Formerly he shouldered his musket, and marched at the sound of the drum ; now, he carries a halberd in the clerical ceremonies before the chapitre. This man, who speaks to travelers of Charlemagne, has Napoleon nearest his heart. When he spoke of the battles in which he had fought, of his old comrades, and of his colonel, the tears streamed from his eyes. He knew that I was a Frenchman; and, on my leaving, said, with a solemnity which I shall never forget—

"You can say, Sir, that you saw at Aix-la-Chapelle an old soldier of the 36th Swiss regiment."

Then, a moment afterwards, added—

"You can also state that he belongs to three nations—Prussian by birth ; Swiss by profession ; but his whole heart is French."

On quitting the chapel I was so much absorbed in reflection, that I all but passed a lovely facade of the fourteenth century, ornamented with the statues of seven emperors. I was awoke from my reverie by the sudden bursts of laughter which escaped from two travelers, the elder of whom, I was told in the morning by my landlord, was

M. le Comte d'A., of the most noble family of Artois.

" Here are names!" they cried. " It certainly required a revolution to form such names as these. Le Capitaine Lasoupe, and Colonel Graindorge."

My poor Swiss had spoken to them, as he did to me, about his old captain and colonel, for they were so called.

A few minutes afterwards I was on my way to the Hotel-de-Ville, the supposed birthplace of Charlemagne, which, like the chapel, is an edifice made of five or six others. In the middle of the court there is a fountain of great antiquity, with a bronze statue of Charlemagne. To the left and right are two others—both surmounted with eagles, their heads half turned towards the grave and tranquil emperor.

The evening was approaching. I had passed the whole of the day among these grand and austere *souvenirs;* and, therefore, deemed it essential to take a walk in the open fields, to breathe the fresh air, and to watch the rays of the declining sun. I wandered along some dilapidated walls, entered a field, then some beautiful alleys, in one of which I seated myself. Aix-la-Chapelle lay extended before me, partly hid by the shades of evening, which were falling around. By degrees the fogs gained the roofs

of the houses, and shrouded the town steeples;
then nothing was seen but two huge masses—the
Hotel-de-Ville and the chapel. All the emotions,
all the thoughts and visions which flitted across
my mind during the day, now crowded upon me.
The first of the two dark objects was to me only
the birthplace of a child; the second was the
resting-place of greatness. At intervals, in the
midst of my reverie, I imagined that I saw the
shade of this giant, whom we call Charlemagne,
developing itself between this great cradle and
still greater tomb.

CHAPTER X.

COLOGNE—THE BANKS OF THE RHINE—ANDER-NACH.

Duez.—Cathedral of Cologne.—The Peasantry.—The Strolling
Musician.—Personifiers of the gods Goulu, Gluton, Gonifre,
and Gouliaf.—Dome of the Cathedral of Cologne.—Epitaph.
—Tomb of the Three Wise Men of the East.—Destiny.—
The Hotel-de-Ville. — The Three Bas-Reliefs. — The Epic
Poet of Cologne.—Cologne at Night.—Time and its Effects.

THE sun had set when we reached Cologne.
I gave my luggage to a porter, with orders to carry it to an hotel at Duez, a little town
on the opposite side of the Rhine ; and directed
my steps towards the cathedral. Rather than
ask my way, I wandered up and down the narrow streets, which night had all but obscured.
At last I entered a gateway leading to a court,
and came out on an open square—dark and deserted. A magnificent spectacle now presented
itself. Before me, in the fantastic light of a
crépusculaire sky, rose, in the midst of a group
of low houses, an enormous black mass, studded
with pinnacles and belfries. A little farther was
another, not quite so broad as the first, but
higher ; a kind of square fortress, flanked at its
angles with four long detached towers, having

on its summit something resembling a huge feather. On approaching, I discovered that it was the cathedral of Cologne.

What appeared like a large feather was a crane, to which sheets of lead were appended, and which, from its workable appearance, indicated to passers-by that this unfinished temple may one day be completed; that the dream of Engelbert de Berg, which was realized under Conrad de Hochsteden, may, in an age or two, be the greatest cathedral in the world. This incomplete Iliad sees Homers in futurity.

The church was shut. I surveyed the steeples, and was startled at their dimensions. What I had taken for towers are the projections of the buttresses. Though only the first story is completed, the building is already nearly as high as the towers of Notre Dame at Paris. Should the spire, according to the plan, be placed upon this monstrous trunk, Strasburg would be, comparatively speaking, small by its side. It has always struck me that nothing resembles ruin more than an unfinished edifice. Briars, saxifrages, and pellitories— indeed, all weeds that root themselves in the crevices and at the base of old buildings— have besieged these venerable walls. Man only constructs what Nature in time destroys.

All was quiet ; there was no one near to

break the prevailing silence. I approached the facade, as near as the gate would permit me, and heard the countless shrubs gently rustling in the night breeze. A light which appeared at a neighboring window, cast its rays upon a group of exquisite statues — angels and saints, reading or preaching, with a large open book before them. Admirable prologue for a church, which is nothing else than the Word made marble, brass or stone! Swallows have fearlessly taken up their abode here, and their simple yet curious masonry contrasts strangely with the architecture of the building.

This was my first visit to the cathedral of Cologne.

By-the-by, I have told nothing of the road between it and Aix-la-Chapelle. In fact, very little can be said ; — a green plain, with an occasional oak and a few poplar-trees, alone meet the eye. In the villages, the old female peasants, enveloped in long mantles, walk about like spectres ; while the young, clothed in short *jupons*, are seen on their knees, washing the door-steps. As for the men, they are decorated with blue smock-frocks and high-crowned hats, as if they were the peasants of a constitutional country.

Scarcely a single person was seen on the road ; the inclemency of the weather was, perhaps, the cause. A poor strolling musician passed — a stick in one hand, and his cornet-à-piston in the other. He was clothed in a blue coat, a fancy waistcoat, and white trousers, with bottoms turned up as high as the legs of his boots. The *pauvre diable*, from the knees upwards, was fitted out for a ball; his lower extremities, however, were better suited for the road. In a little square village, in front of an *auberge*, I admired four jolly-looking travelers seated before a table loaded with flesh, fish and wines. One was drinking, another cutting, a third eating, a fourth devouring—like four personifications of Voraciousness and Gourmandism. It seemed to me as if I beheld the gods Goulu, Glouton, Gonifre, and Gouliaf, seated round a mountain of eatables.

The following morning I again visited the dome of the cathedral of Cologne. I examined the windows of this magnificent edifice, which are of the time of Maximilian, painted with all the extravagance of the German Renaissance. On one of them is a representation of the genealogy of the Holy Virgin. At the bottom of the picture, Adam, in the costume of an emperor, is lying upon his back. A large tree, which fills the whole pane, is growing out of his stomach, and on the branches appear all

the crowned ancestors of Mary : David playing the harp, Solomon in pensiveness ; and at
the top of the tree a flower opens, and discloses the Virgin carrying the infant Jesus.

A few steps farther on I read this epitaph,
which breathes sorrow and resignation :

> " Inclitvs ante fvi comes emvndvs,
> Vocitatvs, hic dece prostratvs, sub
> Tegor vt volvi. Frishem, sancte,
> Mevm fero, petre, tibi comitatvm
> Et mihi redde statvm, te precor,
> Ethcrevm Hæc. Lapidvm massa
> Comitis complectitvr ossa."

I entered the church and was struck with the
choir. There are pictures of all epochs and
of all forms ; innumerable marble statues of
bishops ; chevaliers of the time of the crusades, their dogs lying lovingly at their feet ;
apostles clothed in golden robes ; and tapestries painted from the designs of Rubens.
Everything, it must be said, is shamefully demolished. If some one constructed the exte-
rior of the cathedral of Cologne, I do not
know who has demolished the interior. There
is not a tomb entire, the figures being either
broken off or mutilated. The flies revel on
the venerable face of the Archbishop Philip of
Heinsburg, and the man called Conrad of
Hochsteden, the founder of the church, like
Gulliver, in the Lilliputian tale, cannot at

present crush the spiders that knit him to the ground. Alas! the bronze arm is nothing to the arm of flesh. I observed, in an obscure corner, the dismantled statue of an old man with a long beard; I believe it is that of Michael Angelo.

I will now mention the most venerable structure which this church contains: that of the famed tomb of the Three Wise Men of the East.

The room is of marble, is rather large, and represents the styles of Louis the Thirteenth and Louis the Fourteenth. On raising our eyes, we perceive a *bas-relief* representing the adoration of the three kings, and, underneath, the inscription :

> " Corpora ranctorum recubant hic terna magorum,
> Ex his sublatum nihil est alibive locatum."

This, then, is the resting place of the three poetic kings of the east. Indeed, there is no legend that pleases me so much as this of the *Mille et Une Nuits*. I approached the tomb, and perceived, in the shade, a massive *reliquaire*, sparkling with pearls, diamonds, and other precious stones, which seemed to relate the history of these three kings, *ab oriente venerunt*. In front of the tomb are three lamps, the one bearing the name of Gasper, the other Melchior, and the third Balthazar. It is an ingenious idea to have — somehow illuminated — the names of the three wise men in front of the sepulchre.

On leaving, something pierced the sole of my boot. I looked downwards, and found that it was a large nail projecting from a square of black marble, upon which I was walking. After examining the stone, I remembered that Mary of Medicis had desired that her heart should be placed under the pavement of the cathedral of Cologne, and before the tomb of the three kings. Formerly a bronze or brass plate, with an inscription, covered it; but when the French took Cologne, some revolutionist, or perhaps a rapacious brazier, seized it, as had been done by many others; for a host of brass nails, projecting from the marble, bespeak depredations of a similar nature. Alas, poor queen! She first saw herself effaced from the heart of Louis the Thirteenth, her son; then from the remembrance of Richelieu, her creature; and now she is effaced from the earth.

How strange are the freaks of destiny! Mary de Medicis, widow of Henry the Fourth, exiled and abandoned, had a daughter, Henriette, widow of Charles the First, who died at Cologne in 1642, in the house where, sixty-five years before, Rubens, her painter, was born.

The dome of Cologne, when seen by day, appeared to me to have lost a little of its sublimity; it no longer had what I call *la grandeur crépusculaire* that the evening lends to huge objects; and I must say that the cathedral of Beauvais, which is scarcely known, is not inferior, either in size or in detail, to the cathedral of Cologne.

The Hotel-de-Ville, situated near the cathedral, is one of those singular edifices which have been built at different times, and which consist of all the styles of architecture seen in ancient buildings. The mode in which these edifices have been built forms rather an interesting study. Nothing is regular—no fixed plan has been drawn out—all has been built as necessity required.

Thus the Hotel-de-Ville, which has, probably, some Roman cave near its foundation, was, in 1250, only a structure similar to those of our edifices built with pillars. For the convenience of the night-watchman, and in order to sound the alarum, a steeple was required, and in the fourteenth century a tower was built. Under Maximilian a taste for elegant structures was everywhere spread, and the bishops of Cologne, deeming it essential to dress their city-house in new raiments, engaged an Italian architect, a pupil, probably, of old Michael Angelo, and

a French sculptor, who adjusted on the blackened facade of the thirteenth century a tri-
umphant and magnificent porch. A few years
expired, and they stood sadly in want of a
promenoir by the side of the Registry. A back
court was built, and galleries erected, which
were sumptuously enlivened by heraldry and
bas-reliefs. These I had the pleasure of seeing;
but, in a few years, no person will have the
same gratification, for, without anything being done to prevent it, they are fast falling
into ruins. At last, under Charles the Fifth,
a large room for sales and for the assemblies of
the citizens was required, and a tasteful building of stone and brick was added. Thus a
corps of the thirteenth century, a belfry of the
fourteenth, a porch and back-court of the time
of Maximilian, and a hall of that of Charles the
Fifth, linked together in an original and pleasing manner, form the Hotel-de-Ville of Cologne.

I went up to the belfry; and under a gloomy
sky, which harmonized with the edifice and with
my thoughts, I saw at my feet the whole of this
admirable town.

From Thurmchen to Bayenthurme, the town,
which extends upwards of a league on the
banks of the river, displays a whole host of windows and facades. In the midst of roofs, turrets and gables, the summits of twenty-four

churches strike the eye, all of different styles, and each church, from its grandeur, worthy of the name of cathedral. If we examine the town *en détail,* all is stir, all is life. The bridge is crowded with passengers and carriages ; the river is covered with sails. Here and there clumps of trees caress, as it were, the houses blackened by time ; and the old stone hotels of the fifteenth century, with their long frieze of sculptured flowers, fruit and leaves, upon which the dove, when tired, rests itself, relieve the monotony of the slate roofs and brick fronts which surround them.

Round this great town — mercantile from its industry, military from its position, marine from its river — is a vast plain that borders Germany, which the Rhine crosses at different places, and is crowned on the northeast by historic *croupes* — that wonderful nest of legends and traditions, called the " Seven Mountains." Thus Holland and its commerce, Germany and its poetry — like the two great aspects of the human mind, the positive and the ideal — shed their light upon the horizon of Cologne ; a city of business and of meditation.

After descending from the belfry, I stopped in the yard before a handsome porch of the Renaissance, the second story of which is formed of a series of small triumphal arches,

5

with inscriptions. The first is dedicated to
Cæsar; the second to Augustus; the third to
Agrippa, the founder of Cologne; the fourth to
Constantine, the Christian emperor; the fifth
to Justine, the great legislator; and the sixth
to Maximilian. Upon the facade, the poetic
sculptor has chased three *bas-reliefs*, representing the three lion-combatants, Milo of Crotona, Pepin-le-Bref, and Daniel. At the two
extremities he has placed Milon de Crotone,
attacking the lions by strength of body; and
Daniel subduing the lions by the power of
mind. Between these is Pepin-le-Bref, con-
quering his ferocious antagonist with that mixture of moral and physical strength which dis-
tinguishes the soldier. Between pure strength
and pure thought, is courage; between the
athlete and the prophet—the hero.

Pepin, sword in hand, has plunged his left
arm, which is enveloped in his mantle, into
the mouth of the lion: the animal stands, with
extended claws, in that attitude which in heraldry represents the lion rampant. Pepin at-
tacks it bravely and vanquishes. Daniel is
standing motionless, his arms by his side, and
his eyes lifted up to Heaven, the lions lovingly
rolling at his feet. As for Milo de Crotona,
he defends himself against the lion, which is
in the act of devouring him. His blind pre-

sumption has put too much faith in muscle,
in corporeal strength. These three *bas-reliefs*
contain a world of meaning; the last produces
a powerful effect. It is Nature avenging herself on the man whose only faith is in brute
force.

As I was about to leave the town-house—this
spacious building, this dwelling, rich in legendary lore as well as in historical facts—a man,
in appearance older than he actually was,
crooked from disposition more than from the
influence of age, crossed the yard. The person who conducted me to the belfry, in pointing him out, said :

" That man is a poet: he has composed several epics against Napoleon, against the revolution of 1830, and against the French. The
last, his *chef d'œuvre*, beseeches an architect to
finish the church of Cologne in the same style
as the Pantheon in Paris."

Epics ! granted ! Nevertheless, this man, or
poet, is the most unwashed-looking animal that
ever I put eyes upon. I do not think we have
anything in France that will bear a comparison
with the epic poet of Cologne.

To make up for the opinion which this
strange - looking animal had formed of us, a
little old man, with a quick eye, came out of
a barber's shop, in one—I do not know which

—of the dark and obscure streets, and guessing my country, from my appearance, came to me, shouting out :

" Monsieur, Monsieur, fous, Francais! oh, les Francais! ran! plan! plan! plan! ran, tan, plan! la querre à toute le monde! Prafes! Prafes! Napoleon, n'est-ce pas? La querre à toute l'Europe! Oh, les Francais, pien Prafes, Monsieur. La paionette au qui à tous ces Priciens, eine ponnea quilpite gomme à Iéna. Prafo les Francais! ran! plan! plan!"

I must admit that this harrangue pleased me. France is great in the recollection and in the hopes of these people. All on the banks of the Rhine love us—I had almost said, wait for us.

In the evening, as the stars were shining, I took a walk upon the side of the river opposite to Cologne. Before me was the whole town, with its innumerable steeples figuring in detail upon the pale western sky. To my left rose, like the giant of Cologne, the high spire of St. Martin's, with its two towers; and, almost in front, the sombre abside-cathedral, with its many sharp-pointed spires, resembling a monstrous hedgehog, the crane forming the tail, and near the base two lights, which appeared like two eyes sparkling with fire. Nothing disturbed the stillness of the night but the rustling

of the waters at my feet, the heavy tramp of
a horse's hoofs upon the bridge, and the sound
of a blacksmith's hammer. A long stream of
fire that issued from the forge caused the adjoining windows to sparkle ; then, as if hastening to its opposite element, disappeared in the
water.

From this grand and sombre *ensemble,* my
thoughts took a melancholy turn, and, in a
kind of reverie, I said to myself, " The *germaine*
city has disappeared—the city of Agrippa is no
longer—but the town of St. Engelbert still
stands. How long will it be so? Decay, more
than a thousand years since, seized upon the
temple built by Saint Helena ; the church constructed by the Archbishop Anno is fast de-
caying. Cologne is demolished by its river.
Scarcely a day passes but some old stone, some
ancient relic, is detached by the commotion of
the steamboats. A town is not situated with
impunity upon the great artery of Europe.
Cologne, though not so old as Treves or So-
leure, has already been thrice deformed and
transformed, by the rapid and violent change
of ideas to which it has been subjected. All
is changing. The spirit of *positivism* and *utili-
tarianism*—for which the grovelers of the present day are such strong advocates—penetrates

and destroys. Architecture, old and reverential, gives way to modern *"good taste."* Alas!
old cities are fast disappearing.

CHAPTER XI.

APROPOS OF THE HOUSE " IBACH."

Man's Insignificancy.—The House Ibach.—Marie de Medicis, Richelieu, and Louis the Thirteenth.

WHAT Nature does, perhaps Nature knows; but one thing is certain, and I am not the only one who says so, that men know not what they do. Often in confronting history with the material world, in the midst of those comparisons which my mind draws between the events hidden by God and which time and creation partly disclose, I have secretly shuddered, when thinking that the forests, the lakes, the mountains, the sky, the stars, and the ocean, are things clear and terrible, abounding in light and full of science, and look, as it were, in disdain upon man—that haughty, presumptuous thing, whose arm is linked to impotence—that piece of vanity, blind in its own ignorance. The tree may be conscious of its fruit; but, to me, man knows nothing of his destiny.

The life of man and his understanding are at the mercy of a Divine power, called by some, Providence,—by others, Chance, which blends, combines, and decomposes all; which conceals its workings in the clouds, and discloses the results in open day. We think we do one thing, whilst we do another, *urceus exit.* History affords copious proofs of this. When the husband of Catherine de Medicis, and the lover of Diane de Poitiers, allowed himself to be allured by Philippe Due, the handsome *Piémontaise,* it was not only Diane d'Angouleme that he engendered, but he brought about the reconciliation of his son Henry the Third with his cousin Henry the Fourth. When Charles the Second of England hid himself, after the battle of Worcester, in the trunk of an oak, he only thought of concealment—something more was the result; he named a constellation "The Royal Oak," and gave Halley the opportunity of detracting from the fame of Tycho. Strange that the second husband of Madame de Maintenon in revoking the Edict of Nantes, and the parliament of 1688 in expelling James the Second, should bring about the singular battle of Almanza, where, face to face, were the French army, commanded by an Englishman, Marshal Berwick, and the English army, commanded by a Frenchman, Ruvigny, Lord Galloway. If Louis the Thirteenth had not died on the 14th of May, 1643, it would never have struck the old Count de Fontana to attack Rocroy, which gave an heroic prince of twenty-two the glorious opportunity of making the Duke d'Enghien the great Condé.

In the midst of all these strange and striking facts which load our chronologies, what singular and unforeseen occurrences! what formidable counter-blows! In 1664, Louis the Fourteenth, after the offense done to his ambassador, Crequi, caused the Corsicans to be banished from Rome; a hundred and forty years afterwards Buonaparte exiled the Bourbons from France!

What shadows! but still, what light appears in the midst of the darkness! About 1612, when Henry of Montmorency, then about seventeen years of age, saw among the servants of his father a pale and mean-looking menial, Laubespine de Châteauneuf, bowing and scraping before him, who could have whispered in his ears that this page would become under-deacon; that this under-deacon would become the lord-keeper of the great seal; that this keeper of the great seal would preside at the parliament of Toulouse; and that, at the expiration of twenty years, this "deacon-president" would surlily demand from the Pope permission to have his master, Henry the Second, Duke of Montmorency, Marshal of France, and peer of the kingdom, decapitated? When the president of Thou so carefully added his clauses to the ninth edict of Louis the Eleventh, who could have told the monarch that

5*

this very edict, with Laubardemont for a handle, would be the hatchet with which Richelieu would strike off the head of his son?

In the midst of all this chaos there are laws; confusion is only on the surface, order is at the bottom. After long intervals, frightful facts similar to those which astounded our fathers, come like comets, in all their terror, upon ourselves; always the same ambushes—the same misfortunes; always foundering upon the same coasts. The name alone changes—the acts are still committed. A few days before the fatal treaty of 1814, the emperor might have said to his thirteen marshals—

Amen dico vobis quia unus vestrum me traditurus est.

A Cæsar cherishes a Brutus; a Charles the First prevents a Cromwell from going to Jamaica; a Louis the Sixteenth throws obstacles in the way of a Mirabeau, who is desirous of setting out for the Indies; queens whose deeds are characterized by cruelty are punished by ungrateful sons; Agrippas beget Neros, who destroy those who gave them birth; a Mary of Medicis engenders a Louis the Thirteenth, who banishes her.

You, without doubt, remark the strange turn my thoughts have taken—from one idea to another—to these two Italians—to these two women, Agrippina and Mary de Medicis, the

specters of Cologne. About sixteen hundred
years ago, the daughter of Germanicus, mother
of Nero, connected her name and memory with
Cologne, as did, at a later date, the wife of
Henry the Fourth and mother of Louis the
Thirteenth. The first, who was born there, died
by the poniard; the second expired at Cologne,
from the effects of poison.

I visited, at Cologne, the house in which Mary
of France breathed her last—the house Ibach
according to some, and Jabach according to
others; but, instead of relating what I saw, I
will tell the thoughts that flashed across my
mind when there. Excuse me for not giving all
the local details, of which I am so fond; in fact,
I am afraid that I have, ere this, fatigued my
reader with my *festons* and my *astragales*. The
unhappy queen died here, at the age of sixty-
eight, on the 3rd of July, 1642. She was exiled
for eight years from France, had wandered
everywhere, and was very expensive to the
countries in which she stopped. When at Lon-
don, Charles the First treated her with munifi-
cence, allowing her, the three years she resided
there, a hundred pounds sterling per day. Afterwards—I must say it with regret—Paris *returned*
that hospitality to Henrietta, daughter of Henry
the Fourth and widow of Charles the First, by
giving her a garret in the Louvre, where she

often remained in bed for want of the comforts of a fire, anxiously expecting a few louis that the *coadjuteur* had promised to lend her. Her mother, the widow of Henry the Fourth, experienced the same misery at Cologne.

How strange and striking are these details! Marie de Medicis was not long dead when Richelieu ceased to live, and Louis the Thirteenth expired the following year. For what good was the inveterate hatred that existed between these three mortal beings? for what end so much intrigue, quarreling, and persecution?— God alone knows. All three died almost at the same hour.

There is something remaining of a mysterious nature about Mary de Medicis. I have always been horrified at the terrible sentence that the President Henault, probably without intention, wrote upon this queen :

Elle ne fut pas assez surprise de la mort de Henri IV.

I must admit that all this tends to shed a luster upon that admirable epoch, the glorious reign of Louis the Fourteenth. The darkness that obscured the beginning of that century contrasted admirably with the brilliancy of its close. Louis the Fourteenth was not only, as Richelieu, powerful, but he was majestic ; not only, as Cromwell, great, but in him was serenity. Louis the Fourteenth was not, perhaps, the genius in the master, but genius surrounded him. This may lessen a king in the eyes of some, but it adds to the glory of his reign. As for me, as you already know, I love that which is absolute, which is perfect; and therefore have always had a profound respect for this grave and worthy prince, so well born, so much loved, and so well surrounded; a king in his cradle, a king in the tomb; true sovereign in every acceptation of the word; central monarch of civilization; pivot of Europe; seeing, so to speak, from tour to tour, eight popes, five sultans, three emperors, two kings of Spain, three kings of Portugal, four kings and one queen of England, three kings of Denmark, one queen and two kings of Sweden, four kings of Poland, and four czars of Muscovy, appear, shine forth, and disappear around his throne; polar star of an entire age, who, during seventy-two years, saw all the constellations majestically perform their evolutions round him.

CHAPTER XII.

A FEW WORDS RESPECTING THE WALDRAF MUSEUM.

Schleis Kotten—"Stretching-out-of-the-hand System," or, Traveling Contingencies.—Recapitulation.

BESIDES the cathedral, the Hotel-de-Ville, and the Ibach House, I visited Schleis Kotten, the vestiges of the subterranean aqueduct which, at the time of the Romans, led from Cologne to Travers. Traces of it are at the present day to be seen in thirty-two villages. In Cologne I inspected the Waldraf Museum, and am almost tempted to give you an inventory of all I saw; but I will spare you. Suffice it to know, that if I did not find the war-chariot of the ancient Germans, the famed Egyptian mummy, or the grand culverin founded at Cologne in 1400, I saw a very fine sarcophagus, and the armory of Bernard Bishop of Galen. I was also shown an enormous cuirass, which was said to have been the property of Jean de Wert, a general of the empire; but I sought in vain for his sword, which measured eight feet and a half in length; his immense pike, likened to the pine of Polyphemus; and his large helmet, that, as it is said, took two men to raise it.

The pleasure of seeing all these curiosities—
museums, churches, town-houses, &c.—is alloyed
by the everlasting extended hand—pay, pay.
Upon the borders of the Rhine, as at other
places much frequented, the stranger is obliged
to have his hand in constant communion with
his pocket. The purse of the traveler—that
precious article—is to him everything, since hospitality is no longer seen receiving the weary
traveler with soft words and cordial looks. I
will give you an idea of the extent to which the
stretching-out-of-the-hand is carried on among
the *intelligents naturels* of this country. Remember, there is no exaggeration—only the
truth.

On entering a town, an understrapper ascer-
tains the hotel that you intend putting up at,
asks for your passport, takes it, and puts it into
his pocket. The horses stop; you look round,
and find that you are in a courtyard—that your
present journey is terminated. The driver, who
has not exchanged a word with any one during
the journey, alights, opens the door, and extends his hand with an air of modesty—" Remember the driver." A minute elapses: the
postilion presents himself, and makes an ha-
rangue, which signifies, " Don't forget me." The
luggage is uncorded ; a tall, fleshless animal sets
your portmanteau gently upon the ground, with

your nightcap on the top of it ; so much trouble "must be rewarded." Another creature, more curious perhaps than the latter, puts your chattels upon a wheelbarrow, asks the name of the hotel you have fixed upon, then runs before you, pushing his shapeless machine. No sooner arrived at the hotel than the host approaches, and begins a dialogue, which ought to be written in all languages upon the doors of the respective auberges.

"Good day, sir."

"If you have a spare room, I should like to engage it."

"Very well, sir. Thomas, conduct the gentleman to No. 4."

"I should like something to eat."

"Immediately, sir, immediately."

You go to No. 4, where you find your luggage has arrived. A man appears; it is the person who conveyed the luggage to the hotel. "The porter, sir." A second makes his appearance; what the devil does he want? It is the person who carried your luggage into the room. You say to him—

"Very well; I shall pay you, on leaving, with the other servants."

"Monsieur," the man replies, with a supplicating air, "I don't belong to the hotel."

There is no alternative—"disburse." You

take a walk; a handsome church presents itself. You cannot think of passing it: no, no, you must go in, for it is not every day you meet such a structure; you walk round, gazing at everything; at last a door meets your view. Jesus says, "*Compelle intrare;*" the priests ought to keep the doors open, but the beadles shut them, in order to gain a few sous. An old woman, who has perceived your embarrassment, comes and shows you a bell by the side of a small wicket; you ring, the wicket is opened, and the beadle stands before you.

"Can I see the interior of the church?"

"Certainly," the old man replies, a sort of grim smile lighting up his grave countenance.

He draws out a bunch of keys, and directs his steps towards the principal entrance. Just as you are about to go in, something seizes you by the skirts of your coat; you turn round; it is the obliging old woman, whom you have forgotten, ungrateful wretch! to reward—"pay!" You at last find yourself in the interior of the church; you contemplate, admire, and are struck with wonder.

"Why is that picture covered with a green cloth?"

"Because," the beadle replies, "it is the most beautiful picture in the church."

"What!" you say, in astonishment, "the best

picture hidden ; elsewhere it is exposed to view. Who is it by ? "

" Rubens."

" I should like to see it."

The beadle leaves you, and in a few minutes returns with an old pensive-looking individual by his side ; it is the churchwarden. This worthy personage presses a spring, the curtain draws, and you behold the picture. The painting seen, the curtain closes, and the churchwarden bows significantly—" Pay, pay." On continuing your walk in the church, preceded by the beadle, you arrive at the door of the choir, before which a man has taken up his stand in " patient expectation." It is a Swiss who has the charge of the choir. You walk round it, and, on leaving, your attentive cicerone graciously salutes you—" Only a trifle." You find yourself again with the beadle, and soon after pass before the sacristy. O, wonder of wonders ! the door is open. You enter, and find a sexton. The beadle retires, for the other must be left alone with his prey. The sexton smiles, shows you the urns, the ecclesiastical ornaments and decorated windows, bishops' mitres, and, in a box, a skeleton of some saint dressed as a troubadour. You have seen the sacristy, therefore " must pay." The beadle again appears, and leads you to the ladder that conducts to the

tower. A view from the steeple must be truly
delightful. You decide on going up. The
beadle pushes a door open; you climb up about
thirty steps, then you find that a door which is
locked prevents you proceeding farther. You
look back, and are surprised that the beadle is
no longer with you—that you are alone. What's
to be done? You knock; a face appears; it is
that of the bellman. He opens the door, for
which kind action—"Pay." You proceed on
your way—are delighted to find yourself alone—
that the bellman has not followed. You then
begin to enjoy the pleasure of solitude, and
arrive with a light heart at the high platform of
the tower.

You look about, come and go, admire the
blue sky, the smiling country, and the immense horizon. Suddenly you perceive an unknown animal walking by your side: then your
ears are dinned with things you know, and, perhaps, care little about. It turns out to be the
explicateur, who fills the high office of explaining
to the stranger the magnificence of the steeple,
the church, and the surrounding country. This
man is ordinarily a stutterer, sometimes deaf;
you do not listen to him; you forget him, in
contemplating the churches, the streets, the
trees, the rivers, and the hills. When you have
seen all, you think of descending, and direct

your steps to the top of the ladder. The bell-man is there before you—" Pay."

"Very well," you say, fingering your purse, which is momentarily dissolving; "how much must I give you?"

"I am charged two francs for each person, which sum goes to the church revenue; but, Sir, you must give me something for my trouble."

You descend; the beadle makes his appearance, and conducts you with respect to the door of the church. So much trouble cannot fail to be well rewarded.

You return to your hotel, and have scarcely entered when you see a person approaching you with a familiar air, and who is totally a stranger to you. It is the understrapper who took your passport, and who now returns with it—to be paid. You dine; the hour of your departure comes, and a servant brings you in the bill—Pay; also a consideration for the trouble of taking the money. An ostler carries your portmanteau to the diligence—you must remember him. You get into the vehicle; you set off; night falls: you begin the same course to-morrow.

Let us recapitulate. Something to the driver, a trifle to the postilion, the porter, the man who does not belong to the hotel, to the old woman, to Rubens, to the Swiss, to the sexton, to the bellman, to the church revenue, to the beadle, to the passport-keeper, to the servants, and to the ostler. How many *pays* do you call that in a day? Remember, every one must be silver; copper is looked upon here with the greatest contempt, even by a bricklayer's laborer.

To this ingenious people the traveler is a sack of crowns, which the good inhabitants, in order to reduce the bulk as soon as possible, are ever sweating. The government itself occasionally claims a share of the spoil; it takes your trunk and portmanteau, places them upon its shoulders, and offers you its hand. In large towns the porters pay to the royal treasury twelve sous two liards for each traveler. I was not a quarter of an hour at Aix-la-Chapelle before I had given my mite to the King of Prussia.

CHAPTER XIII.

ANDERNACH.

A view from Andernach.—Village of Luttersdorf.—Cathedral.—
Its Relics.—Andernach Castle.—Inscription.—The Tomb of
Hoche.—Gothic Church and Inscription.

ANDERNACH, where I have been stopping
for the last three days, is an ancient muni-
cipal town, situated upon the banks of the
Rhine. The *coup-d'œil* from my window is truly
charming. Before me, at the foot of a high hill,
which obscures from my view part of the blue
sky, is a handsome tower of the thirteenth century; to my right the Rhine, and the charming
little white village of Leutersdorf, half hidden
among the trees; and to my left the four steeples
of a magnificent church. Under my window
children are playing, the noise of their prattlings
mingling with the quacking of geese and the
chuckling of hens.

I visited the church on the day of my arrival,
the interior of which is, notwithstanding the
hideous manner that some one has plastered it,
rather handsome. The Emperor Valentinian,
and a child of Frederick Barberousse, were interred in this church, but neither inscriptions

nor tombstones indicated the place where they were buried. Our Saviour at the tomb; a few statues, life size, of the fifteenth century, and a chevalier of the sixteenth, leaning against a wall; several figures; the fragments of a mausoleum of the Renaissance, were all that the smiling hump-backed bellringer could show me for a little piece of silvered copper which passes here for thirty sous.

I must tell a little adventure which I had— an incident that has left on my mind the impression of a sombre dream.

On leaving the church I walked round the city. The sun was setting behind the high hills that, in seeming pride and pristine glory, look down upon the Rhine, on the imperial tomb of Valentinian, on the abbey of Saint Thomas, and on the old walls of the feudal town of the electors of Treves.

I pursued my way by the side of the moat that skirts the dilapidated walls, the fallen stones of which serve as seats and tables for half-naked urchins to play upon, and in the evening for young men to tell their fair *bergères* the achings of their wounded hearts. The formidable castle, that was once the defense of Andernach, is now an immense ruin; and the court, once the seat of war, is now covered with grass, upon which women bleach in summer the cloth that they have woven in winter.

After leaving the outer gate of Andernach, I found myself on the banks of the Rhine. The night was calm and serene, and nature had lulled itself to sleep. Shepherdesses came to drink from the clear stream, then in mirth ran away to hide themselves among the osieries. Before me a white village was all but lost in the distance, and towards the east, at the extreme border of the horizon, the full moon, red and round like the eye of a Cyclop, appeared between two clouds.

How often have I walked thus, unconscious of all save the beauties which nature presented, alive only to that dame who has so great a sway over the sensitive mind! I knew not where I was, nor where I was straying; and when I awoke from my reverie I found myself at the foot of a rising ground, crowned at the summit by some stonework. I approached, and was somewhat startled on finding a tomb. Whose was it? I walked round, trying to discover the name of the person whom it memorialized, and at last perceived the following inscription in brass letters:

L'armée de Sambre et Meuse à son Général en Chef.

Above these two lines I saw, by the light of the moon, which was shining brightly, the name— HOCHE. The letters had been taken away, but had left their imprint on the granite.

That name, in this place, at such an hour, and seen by such a light, had a strange, an inexpressible effect upon me. Hoche was always a favorite of mine: he, like Marceau, was one of those young men who preluded Buonaparte in an attempt which was all but successful. This, then, I thought, is the resting-place of Hoche, and the well-remembered date of the 18th of April, 1797, flashed across my memory.

I looked around me, endeavoring, but in vain, to identify the spot. To the north was a vast plain; to the south, about the distance of a gunshot, the Rhine; and at my feet, at the base of this tomb, was a small village.

At that moment a man passed a few steps from the monument. I asked him the name of the village, and he answered, while disappearing behind a hedge, "Weiss Thurm."

These two words signify White Tower. I then remembered *Turris Alba* of the Romans, and was proud to find that Hoche had died in an illustrious place. It was here that Cæsar, two thousand years ago, first crossed the Rhine.

It is impossible for me to tell my inward feelings while contemplating the tomb of this great man. Compassion seized my heart. Can such be the resting place of this illustrious warrior, seemingly forgotten by his countrymen, unheeded by the stranger! This tomb, built by

his army, is at the mercy of the passer-by. The
French General sleeps in a bean-field far from
his country, and Prussian bricklayers make whatever use it pleases them of this tomb!

It seemed to me as if I heard a voice coming
from the heap of stones, saying, "France must
again possess the Rhine."

Andernach is a lovely place, with which I was
truly delighted. From the top of the hills the
eye embraces an immense circle, extending from
Sibengeburge to the crests of Ehrenbreitstein.
Here there is not a stone of an edifice that has
not its *souvenir*, not a single view in the country
that has not its beauties and its graces; and,
what is more, the countenances of the inhabitants have that frank and open expression
which fails not to create delight in the heart of
the traveler. Andernach is a charming town,
notwithstanding Andernach is a deserted place.
Nobody goes where History, Nature, and Poetry
abound; Coblentz, Bade, and Mannheim are
now the exclusive resort of *sophisticated* tour-
ists.

I went a second time to the church. The
Byzantine decoration of the steeples is rich, and
of a taste at once rude and exquisite. The
chapitres of the southern portal are very curious; there is a representation of the Cruci-
fixion still perfectly visible upon the pediment,

and on the facade a *bas-relief*, representing Jesus on his knees, with His arms widely extended: on all sides of him lie scattered about, as if in a frightful dream, the mantle of derision, the sceptre of reeds, the crown of thorns, the rod, the pincers, the hammer, the nails, the ladder, the spear, the sponge filled with gall, the sinister profile of the hardened thief, the livid countenance of Judas; and before the eyes of the Divine Master is the cross, and at a little distance the cock crowing, reminding him of the ingratitude and abandonment of his friend. This last idea is sublime; there is depicted that moral sufferance which is more acute than the physical.

The gigantic shadows of the two steeples darken this sad elegy. Round the bas-relief the sculptor has engraved the following expressive words:

"*O vos omnesqui transitis per viam, attendite et videte si est dolor similis sicut dolor meus.* 1538."

There is another handsome church at Andernach, of Gothic structure, which is now transformed into an immense stable for Prussian cavalry. By the half-open door we perceive a long row of horses, which are lost in the shadows of the chapel. Above the door are the words, "*Sancta Maria, ora pro nobis;*" which is not exactly an apropos inscription for the abode of horses.

CHAPTER XIV.

THE RHINE.

The Rhine at Evening.—Contrast of the Rhine with other Rivers.—The First People who took Possession of the Banks of the Rhine.—Titus and the Twenty-second Legion. —Mysterious Populations of the Rhine. — Civilization.— Pepin-le-Bref, Charlemagne, and Napoleon.

I LOVE rivers; they do more than bear merchandise—ideas float along their surface. Rivers, like clarions, sing to the ocean of the beauty of the earth, the fertility of plans, and the splendor of cities.

Of all rivers, I prefer the Rhine. It is now a year, when passing the bridge of boats at Kehl, since I first saw it. I remember that I felt a certain respect, a sort of adoration, for this old, this classic stream. I never think of rivers— those great works of Nature, which are also great in History,—without emotion.

I remember the Rhone at Valserine; I saw it in 1825, in a pleasant excursion to Switzerland, which is one of the sweet, happy recollections of my early life. I remember with what noise, with what ferocious bellowing, the Rhone precipitated itself into the gulf whilst the frail bridge upon which I was standing was shaking beneath my feet. Ah! well! since that time, the Rhone brings to my mind the idea of a tiger,—the Rhine, that of a lion.

The evening on which I saw the Rhine for the first time, I was impressed with the same idea. For several minutes I stood contemplating this proud and noble river—violent, but not furious; wild, but still majestic. It was swollen, and was magnificent in appearance, and was washing with its yellow mane, or, as Boileau says, its "slimy beard," the bridge of boats. Its two banks were lost in the twilight, and though its roaring was loud, still there was tranquillity.

Yes, the Rhine is a noble river—feudal, republican, imperial—worthy, at the same time, of France and of Germany. The whole history of Europe is combined within its two great aspects—in this flood of the warrior and of the philosopher—in this proud stream, which causes France to bound with joy, and by whose profound murmurings Germany is bewildered in dreams.

The Rhine is unique: it combines the qualities of every river. Like the Rhone, it is rapid; broad, like the Loire; encased, like the Meuse; serpentine, like the Seine; limpid and green, like the Somme; historical, like the Tiber; royal, like the Danube; mysterious, like the Nile;

spangled with gold, like an American river; and like a river of Asia, abounding with phantoms and fables.

Before the commencement of History, perhaps before the existence of man, where the Rhine now is there was a double chain of volcanos, which on their extinction left heaps of lava and basalt lying parallel, like two long walls. At the same epoch the gigantic crystallizations formed the primitive mountains; the enormous alluvions of which the secondary mountains consist were dried up; the frightful heap which is now called the Alps grew gradually cold, and snow accumulated on them, from which two great streams issued, the one,—flowing towards the north, crossed the plains, encountered the sides of the extinguished volcanos, and emptied itself into the ocean; the other, taking its course westward, fell from mountain to mountain, flowed along the side of the block of extinguished volcanos which is now called Ardeche, and was finally lost in the Mediterranean. The first of those inundations is the Rhine, and the second the Rhone.

From historical records we find that the first people who took possession of the banks of the Rhine were the half-savage Celts, who were afterwards named Gauls by the Romans. When Rome was in its glory, Cæsar crossed the Rhine, and shortly afterwards the whole of the river was under the jurisdiction of his empire. When the Twenty-second Legion returned from the siege of Jerusalem, Titus sent it to the banks of the Rhine, where it continued the work of Martius Agrippa. The conquerors required a town to join Melibocus to Taunus; and Moguntiacum, began by Martius, was founded by the Legion, built by Trajan, and embellished by Adrian. Singular coincidence! and which we must note in passing. This Twenty-second Legion brought with it Crescentius, who was the first that carried the Word of God into the Rhingau, and founded the new religion. God ordained that these ignorant men, who had pulled down the last stone of His temple upon the Jordan, should lay the first of another upon the banks of the Rhine. After Trajan and Adrian came Julian, who erected a fortress upon the confluence of the Rhine and the Moselle; then Valentinian, who built a number of castles. Thus, in a few centuries, Roman colonies, like an immense chain, linked the whole of the Rhine.

At length the time arrived when Rome was to assume another aspect. The incursions of the northern hordes were eventually too frequent and too powerful for Rome; so, about the sixth century, the banks of the Rhine were strewed with Roman ruins, as at present with feudal ones.

Charlemagne cleared away the rubbish, built fortresses, and opposed the German hordes; but, notwithstanding all that he did, notwithstanding his desire to do more, Rome died, and the physiognomy of the Rhine was changed.

Already, as I before mentioned, an unperceived germ was sprouting in the Rhingau. Religion, that divine eagle, began to spread its wings, and deposited among the rocks an egg that contained the germ of a world. Saint Apollinaire, following the example of Crescentius, who, in the year 70, preached the Word of God at Taunus, visited Rigomagum. Saint Martin, Bishop of Tours, catechised Confluentia; Saint Materne, before visiting Tongres, resided at Cologne. At Treves, Christians began to suffer the death of martyrdom, and their ashes were swept away by the wind; but these were not lost, for they became seeds, which were germinating in the fields during the passage of the barbarians, although nothing at that time was seen of them.

After an historical period the Rhine became linked with the marvelous. Where the noise of man is hushed, Nature lends a tongue to the nests of birds, causes the caves to whisper, and thousand voices of solitude to murmur: where historical facts cease, imagination gives life to shadows and realities to dreams. Fables took root, grew, and blossomed in the voids of History, like weeds and brambles in the crevices of a ruined palace.

Civilization, like the sun, has its nights and its days, its plentitudes and its eclipses; now it disappears, but soon returns.

As soon as civilization again dawned upon Taunus, there were upon the borders of the Rhine a whole host of legends and fabulous stories. Populations of mysterious beings, who inhabited the now dismantled castles, had held communion with the *belles filles* and *beaux chevaliers* of the place. Spirits of the rocks; black hunters, crossing the thickets upon stags with six horns; the maid of the black fen; the six maidens of the red marshes; Wodan, the god with ten hands; the twelve black men; the raven that croaked its song; the devil who placed his stone at Teufelstein and his ladder at Teufelsleiter, and who had the effrontery to preach publicly at Gernsbach, near the Black Forest, but, happily, the Word of God was heard at the other side of the stream; the demon Urian, who crossed the Rhine at Dusseldorf, having upon his back the banks that he had taken from the sea-shore, with which he intended to destroy Aix-la-Chapelle, but being fatigued with his burden, and deceived by an old woman, he stupidly dropped his load at the imperial city,

6*

where that bank is at present pointed out, and bears the name of Loosberg. At that epoch, which for us was plunged into a penumbra, when magic lights were sparkling here and there, when the rocks, the woods, the valleys, were tenanted by apparitions; mysterious encounters, infernal castles, melodious songs sung by invisible song-stresses; and frightful bursts of laughter emanating from mysterious beings,—these, with a host of other adventures, shrouded in impossibility, and holding on by the heel of reality, are detailed in the legends.

At last these phantoms disappeared as dawn burst in upon them. Civilization again resumed its sway, and fiction gave place to fact. The Rhine assumed another aspect: abbeys and convents increased; churches were built along the banks of the river. The ecclesiastic princes multiplied the edifices in the Rhingau, as the prefects of Rome had done before them.

The sixteenth century approached: in the fourteenth the Rhine witnessed the invention of artillery; and on its bank, at Strasbourg, a printing-office was first established. In 1400 the famous cannon, fourteen feet in length, was cast at Cologne; and in 1472 Vindelin de Spire printed his Bible. A new world was making its appearance; and, strange to say, it was upon the banks of the Rhine that those two mysterious tools with which God unceasingly works out the civilization of man,—the catapult and the book—war and thought,—took a new form.

The Rhine, in the destinies of Europe, has a sort of providential signification. It is the great moat which divides the north from the south. The Rhine for thirty ages, has seen the forms and reflected the shadows of almost all the warriors who tilled the old continent with that share which they call sword. Cæsar crossed the Rhine in going to the south ; Attila crossed it when descending to the north. It was here that Clovis gained the battle of Tolbiac ; and that Charlemagne and Napoleon figured. Frederick Barberousse, Rodolph de Hapsbourg, and Frederick the First, were great, victorious, and formidable when here. For the thinker, who is conversant with History, two great eagles are perpetually hovering over the Rhine—that of the Roman legions, and the eagle of the French regiments.

The Rhine—that noble flood, which the Romans named *Rhenus superbus,* bore at one time upon its surface bridges of boats, over which the armies of Italy, Spain, and France poured into Germany, and which, at a later date, were made use of by the hordes of barbarians when rushing into the ancient Roman world : at another, on its surface it floated peaceably the fir-trees of Murg and of Saint Gall, the prophyry and the marble of Bale, the salt of Karlshall, the leather of Stromberg, the quicksilver of Lansberg, the wine of Johannisberg, the slates of Coab, the cloth and earthenware of Wallendar, the silks and linens of Cologne. It majestically performs its double function of flood of war and flood of peace, having, without interruption, upon the ranges of hills which embank the most notable portion of its course, oak-trees on one side and vine-trees on the other—signifying strength and joy.

For Homer the Rhine existed not; for Virgil it was only a frozen stream—*Frigora Rheni :* for Shakspeare it was the "beautiful Rhine;" for us it is, and will be to the day when it shall become the grand question of Europe, a picturesque river, the resort of the unemployed of Ems, of Baden, and of Spa.

Petrarch visited Aix-la-Chapelle, but I do not think he has spoken of the Rhine.

The left bank belongs naturally to France: Providence, at three different periods, gave it its two banks—under Pepin-le-Bref, Charlemagne, and Napoleon. The empire of Pepin-le-Bref comprised, properly speaking, France, with the exception of Aquitaine and Gascony, and Germany as far as Bavaria. The empire of Charlemagne was twice as large as that of Napoleon.

It is true that Napoleon had three empires, or, more plainly speaking, was emperor in three ways,—immediately and directly of France, and, by his brothers, of Italy, Westphalia, and Holland. Taken in this sense, the empire of Napoleon was at least equal to that of Charlemagne.

These emperors were Titans; they held for a moment the universe in their hands, but Death ultimately caused them to relax their hold.

The Rhine has had four distinct phases—first, the antedeluvian epoch, volcanos; second, the ancient historical epoch, in which Cæsar shone; third, the marvelous epoch, in which Charlemagne triumphed; fourth, the modern historical epoch, when Germany wrestled with France— when Napoleon for a time held his sway.

The Rhine—providential flood—seems to be a symbolical stream. In its windings, in its course, in the midst of all that it traverses, it is, so speaking, the image of civilization to which it has been so useful, and which it will still serve. It flows from Constance to Rotterdam; from the country of eagles to the village of herrings; from the city of popes, of councils, and of emperors, to the counter of the merchant and of the citizen; from the great Alps themselves to that immense body of water which we term *ocean*.

CHAPTER XV.

THE MOUSE.

Velmich.—Legend of the Priest and the Silver Bell.—Giant's Tomb. — Explanation of the Mouse. — The Solitary inhabitants of the Ruin.

ON my leaving Cologne it rained the whole of the morning. I had taken my passage to Andernach by the Stadt Manheim; but had not proceeded far up the Rhine, when suddenly—I do not know by what caprice, for ordinarily upon the lake of Constance the south-west winds, the Favonius of Virgil and of Horace, bring storms —the immense opaque cloud which pended over our heads, burst, and began to disperse itself in all directions. Shortly after, a blue vault appeared; and bright warm rays caused the travelers to leave the cabin and hurry to the deck.

At that moment we passed—with vines on the one side, and oaks on the other—an old and picturesque village on the right bank of the river. It was that of Velmich, above which rose, almost vertically, one of those enormous banks of lava that resemble the cupola in its immeasurable proportions. Upon this volcanic mound stands the ruin of a superb feudal fortress. On the borders of the river a group of young women, busily chatting, were bleaching their linen in the rays of the sun.

This sight was too tempting. I could not pass without paying the ruin a visit; for I knew that it was that of Velmich—the least esteemed and least frequented upon the Rhine.

For the traveler, it is difficult to approach, and, some say, dangerous; for the peasant, it abounds with spectres, and is the subject of frightful tales. It is infested with living flames, which hide themselves by day in subterraneous vaults, and at night become visible on the summit of the round tower. This enormous turret is an immense pit, which descends far beneath the level of the Rhine. A Seigneur of Velmich, called Falkenstein,—a name fatal in the legends, threw into this aperture, unshriven, whomsoever he pleased: it is the troubled souls of those that were thus murdered who inhabit the castle. There were at that epoch, in the steeple of Velmich, a silver bell which was given by Winifred, Bishop of Mayenne, the year 740,—memorable time, when Constantine the Sixth was emperor of Rome. This bell was once rung for the prayers of forty hours, when a lord of Velmich was seriously ill. Falkenstein, who did not believed in God, and who even doubted the existence of the devil, being in want of money, cast

an envious look upon the handsome bell. He
caused it to be taken from the church and
brought to him. The prior of Velmich was much
affected at the sacrilege, and went, in sacerdotal
habiliments, preceded by two children of the
choir bearing the cross, to demand the bell.
Falkenstein burst into a fit of laughter, crying—

"Ah, ah! you wish to have your bell, do you?
Well, you shall have it; and I warrant it never
will leave you more!"

Thereupon, the bell was tied round the priest's
neck, and both were thrown into the pit of the
tower. Then, upon the order of Falkenstein,
large stones were thrown into the pit, filling up
about six feet. A few days afterwards, Falkenstein fell ill; and when night came, the doctor
and the astrologer, who were watching, heard
with terror the knell of the silver bell coming
from the depths of the earth. Next morning
Falkenstein died. Since that time, as regularly
as the years roll over, the silver bell is heard
ringing under the mountains, reminding the inhabitants of the anniversary of the death of
Falkenstein. So runs the legend.

On the neighboring mountain—that on the
other side of the torrent of Velmich—is the
tomb of an ancient giant; for the imagination
of man—he who has seen volcanoes, the great

forges of nature—has put Cyclops wherever the mountains smoked, giving to every Ætna its Polyphemus.

I began to ascend the ruins between the *souvenir* of Falkenstein and that of the giant. I must tell you that the best way was pointed out to me by the children of the village, for which service I allowed them to take some of the silver and copper coins of those people from my purse; things the most fantastic, yet still the most intelligible in the world.

The road is steep, but not at all dangerous, except to people subject to giddiness; or, perhaps, after excessive rains, when the ground and rocks are slippery. One thing sure is, that this ruin has one advantage over others upon the Rhine— that of being less frequented.

No officious person follows you in your ascent; no exhibitor of spectres asks you to "remember him;" no rusty door stops you on your way: you climb, stride over the old ladder, hold on by tufts of grass; no one helps, nor no one annoys you. At the expiration of twenty minutes I reached the summit of the hill, and stopped at the threshold of the ruin. Behind me was a steep ladder formed of green turf; before me, a lovely landscape; at my feet, the village; beyong the village, the Rhine, crowned by sombre

mountains and old castles; and round and above
the mountains, a bright blue sky.

Having taken breath, I began to ascend the
steep staircase. At that instant the dismantled
fortress appeared to me with such a tattered aspect—an aspect so wild and formidable—that I
should not have been the least surprised to have
seen some supernatural form carrying flowers;—
for instance, Gela, the betrothed of Barberousse;
or Hildegarde, the wife of Charlemagne, that
amiable empress, who was well acquainted with
the occult virtues of herbs and minerals, and
whose foot often trod the mountains when she
was in search of medicinal plants. I looked for
a moment towards the north wall, with a sort of
vague desire to see start from the stones a host
of hobgoblins,—which are "all over the north,"
as the gnome said to the Canon of Sayn,—or the
three little old women, singing the legendary
song,—

> "Sur la tombe du géant
> J'ai cueilli trois bris d'orties:
> En fil les ai converties;
> Prenez, ma sœur, ce présent."

But I was forced to content myself without
seeing or even hearing anything except the notes
of a blackbird, perched upon some adjoining
rock.

I entered the ruins. The round tower, although the summit is partly dismantled, is of a

prodigious elevation. On all sides are immense walls with shattered windows, rooms without doors or roofs, floors without stairs, and stairs without chambers. I have often admired the carefulness with which Solitude keeps, incloses, and defends that which man has once abandoned. She barricades and thicksets the threshold with the strongest briers, the most stinging plants, nettles, brambles, thorns—showing more nails and talons than are in a menagerie of tigers.

But Nature is beautiful even in her strangest freaks; and the wild flowers—some in bud, others in blossom, and some garbed in autumnal foliage—present an entanglement at once startling and beautiful. On this side are bluebells and scarlet berries; on that are the hawthorn, gentian, strawberry, thyme, and sloe-tree. To my right is a subterraneous passage, the roof falling in; and to my left is a tower without any visible aperture. Secluded as this spot may seem, the cheerful voices of washerwomen on the Rhine are distinctly heard. I clambered from bush to bush, explored each aperture, and tried to penetrate each vault.

I forgot to tell you that this huge ruin is called the Mouse. I will inform you how it received that appellation:

In the twelfth century there was nothing here

but a small borough, which was watched, and
often molested, by a strong castle called the Cat.
Kuno de Falkenstein, who inherited this paltry
borough, razed it to the ground, and built a
castle much larger than the neighboring one;
declaring that, " henceforth, it should be the
Mouse that would devour the Cat."

He was right. The Mouse, in fact, although
now in ruins, is a redoubtable godmother, with
its haunches of lava and basalt, and entrails
of extinguished volcano, which, with seeming
haughtiness, support it. I do not think that
any person has had occasion to laugh at that
mountain which brought forth the Mouse.

I wandered about the ruins; first in one
room, then in another; admiring at one time
a beautiful turret; now descending into a
cave, groping my way through some subterraneous passage; then finding myself looking
through an aperture that commanded a view
of the Rhine.

The sun at last began to disappear, which
is the time for spectres and phantoms. I was
still in the ruins. Indeed, it seemed to me as
if I had become a wild schoolboy. I wandered
everywhere; I climbed up every acclivity; I
turned over the large stones; I ate wild mul-
berries; I tried by my noise to bring the supernatural inhabitants from their hiding-places;

and, as I trod among the thick grass and herbs,
I inhaled that acerb odor of the plants of old
ruins which I so much loved in my boyhood.

As the sun descended behind the mountains,
I thought of leaving, when I was startled by
something strange moving by my side. I
leaned forward. It was a lizard of an extraordinary size—about nine inches long, with
an immense belly, a short tail, a head like
that of a viper, and black as jet—which was
gliding slowly towards an opening in an old
wall. That was the mysterious and solitary
inhabitant of the ruin—an animal at the same
time real and fabulous—a salamander, which
looked at me with mildness as it entered its
hole.

CHAPTER XVI.

THE MOUSE.

Colossal Profile.—The Duchy of M. de Nassau.—Country Sports :
Their Punishment.—A Mountebank.

I COULD not leave this ruin ; several times
I began to descend, then reascended. Nature, like a smiling mother, indulges us in our
dreams and in our caprices.

At length, when leaving the Mouse, the idea
struck me to apply my ear to the basement
of the large tower. I did so, trusting to hear
some noise, yet scarcely flattering myself that
Winifred's bell would deign to awake itself for
me. At that moment,—O wonder of wonders!
—I heard—yes, heard with mine own ears—a
vague, metallic sound, an indistinct humming
of a bell, gliding through the crepuscule, and,
seemingly, coming from beneath the tower. I
confess that this strange noise brought vividly
to my memory the speech of Hamlet to Ho-
ratio ; but suddenly I was recalled from the
world of chimeras to that of reality. I soon
discovered that it was the Ave Maria of some
village floating with the evening breeze. It
mattered not. All that I had to do was to

believe and say that I heard the mysterious
bell of Velmich tinkling under the mountain.

As I left the north moat, which is now a
thorny ravine, the Giant's Tomb suddenly presented itself. From the point where I stood,
the rock figures, at the base of the mountain,
close to the Rhine, the colossal profile of a
head, hanging backwards, with open mouth.
One is ready to believe that the giant, who,
according to the legend, lies there, crushed under the weight of the mountain, was about to
raise the enormous mass, and that, on his head
appearing between the rocks, an Apollo, or a
St. Michael, put his foot upon the mountain,
and crushed the monster, who expired in that
posture, uttering a fearful shriek, which is lost
in the darkness of forty ages; but the mouth
still remains open.

I must declare, that neither the giant, the
silver bell, nor the spectre of Falkenstein, prevents the vine and weeds mounting from terrace to terrace near the Mouse. So much the
worse for the phantoms of this country of the
grape; for the people do not hesitate to take
the vine that clusters round their dismantled
dwelling to procure themselves the wherewithal
to make wine.

But the stranger, even the most thirsty, must
be cautious how he plucks the fruit, to him for-

bidden. At Velmich we are in the duchy of M. de Nassau, and the laws of Nassau are rigorous respecting such country sports. The delinquent, if caught, is forced to pay a sum equivalent to the depredations or "delights" of all those who are lucky enough to escape. A short time ago an English tourist plucked and ate a plum, for which he had to pay fifty florins.

Wishing to proceed to Saint Goar, which is upon the left bank, I inquired my way of the village mountebank, who gave me directions in a gibberish which, of course, I did not understand; for, instead of going by the road that runs by the river, I took that which leads to the mountain. After walking for a considerable time, I at length came in view of the Rhine; when, through the fog, I saw a group of houses, with faint lights glimmering in the windows. It was St. Goar.

CHAPTER XVII.

SAINT GOAR.

The Cat.—Its Interior.—Fabulous Rock of Lurley.—The Swiss
Valley.—The Fruit Girl.—The Reichenberg.—The Barbers'
Village.— Legend.—The Rheinfels. — Oberwesel. — French
Hussar.—A German Supper.

A WEEK might be very agreeably spent at
St. Goar, which is a neat little town lying
between the Cat and the Mouse. To the left is
the Mouse, half enveloped in the fog of the
Rhine; and to the right is the Cat, a huge
dungeon, with the picturesque village of Saint
Goarshausen, lying at its base. The two formidable castles seem to be casting angry looks across
the country, their dilapidated windows presenting a most hideous aspect. In front, upon the
right bank of the river, and apparently ready to
incite the two adversaries, is the old colossal
spectre palace of the Landgraves of Hesse.

The Rhine at St. Goar, with its sombre em-
bankments, its shadows, its rippling waters, resembles a lake of Jura more than it does a
river.

If we remain in the house, we have all day before us a view of the Rhine, with rafts floating

7

on its surface. Here sailing-vessels, there steamboats, which, when passing, make a noise resembling that of a huge dog when swimming.
In the distance on the opposite bank, under the
shade of some beautiful walnut-trees, we see the
soldiers of M. de Nassau, dressed in red coats
and white trousers, performing their exercise,
while the rolling of the drum of a petty duke
strikes out ear. Under our windows, the women
of St. Goar, with their sky-blue bonnets, pass to
and fro; and we hear the prattling and laughing
of children, who are diverting themselves on the
river's brink.

If we go out we can get across the Rhine for
six sous, the price of a Parisian omnibus; then
amusing ourselves by paying a visit to the Cat
which is an interesting ruin. The interior is
completely dismantled. The lower room of the
tower is at present used as a storehouse. Several
vine-trees twine themselves round it, and even
grow upon the floor of the portait-gallery. In a
small room, the only one that has a window and
door, a picture representing Bohdan Chmielnicki
is nailed to the wall, with two or three portraits
of reigning princes hung round about it.

From the height of the Cat the eye encounters
the famed gulf of the Rhine, called the Bank.
Between the Bank and the square tower of Saint
Goarshausen there is only a narrow passage, the

gulf being on one side, and the rock on the other.
A little beyond the Bank, in a wild and savage
turning, the fabulous rock of Lurley, with its
thousand granite seats, which give it the appearance of a falling ladder, descends into the Rhine.
There is a celebrated echo here, that responds
seven times to all that is said and all that is
sung. If it were not to appear that I wished to
detract from the celebrity of the echo, I would
say that to me the repetition was never above
five times. It is probable that the Oréade of
Lurley, formerly courted by so many princes and
mythological counts, begins to get hoarse and
fatigued. The poor nymph has at present no
more than one admirer who has made himself,
on the opposite side of the Rhine, two chambers
in the rocks, where he passes his days in playing
the horn and in discharging his gun. The man
who gives the echo so much employment, is an
old brave French hussar.

The effect of the echo of Lurley is truly extraordinary: a small boat, crossing the Rhine at
this place, makes a tremendous noise; and,
should we shut our eyes, we might believe that
it was a galley from Malta, with its fifty large
oars, each moved by four galley-slaves.

Before leaving Saint Goarshausen, we must go
and see, in an old street which runs parallel with
the Rhine, a charming little house of the Ger-

man Renaissance. Afterwards we turn to the right, cross a bridge, and enter, amidst the noise of a water-mill, the Swiss Valley, a superb ravine, almost Alpine, formed by the high hill of Petersberg, and by the brow of the Lurley.

The Swiss Valley is certainly a delightful promenade. We ascend acclivities; descend: we meet high villages; plunge into dark and narrow passages, in one of which I saw the ground that had lately been torn up by the tusks of a wild boar; or we proceed along the bottom of the ravine, with rocks resembling the walls of Cyclops on each side. Then, if we draw towards the other road, which abounds with farms and mills, all that meet the eye seem arranged and grouped for Poussin to insert into a corner of his landscape:—a shepherd, half naked, in a field with his flock, contentedly whistling some air: a cart drawn by oxen; and pretty girls with bare feet. I saw one who was indeed charming; she was seated near a fire, drying her fruit, she lifted up her large blue eyes towards heaven—eyes like diamonds, and countenance darkened by the heat of the sun. Her neck, which was partly covered by a collar, was marked with small-pox, and under her chin was a swelling. With that detraction, joined to such beauty, one might have taken her for an Indian idol, squatted near its altar.

We cross a meadow; the hares of the ravine
run here and there, and we suddenly behold, at
the top of a hill, an admirable ruin. It is the
Reichenberg, in which, during the wars of "manual
rights," in the middle age, one of the most
redoubtable of those gentlemen bandits, who
bore the epithet of "the scourge of the country,"
lived. The neighboring village had cause
for lamentation, the emperor had reason for summoning
the brigand to his presence; but the man
of iron, secure in his granite house, heeded him
not, but continued his depredatious, his orgies of
rapine and plunder, and lived excommunicated
by the church, condemned by the Deity, tracked
by the emperor, until his white beard descended
to his stomach. I entered the Reichenberg.
There is nothing in that cave of Homeric thieves
but wild herbs: the windows are all dismantled,
and cows are seen grazing round the ruins.

Behind the hill of the Reichenberg are the
ruins of a town, which has all but disappeared,
and which bore the name of the "BARBERS' VILLAGE."
The following is the account given of
it :

The Devil, wishing to avenge himself on Frederick
Barberousse for his numerous crusades,
took it into his head to have the beard of the
crusader shaved. He made arrangements that
the emperor Barberousse, when passing through

Bacharach, should fall asleep, and, when in that
state, be shaved by one of the numerous barbers
of the village. A tricky fairy, as small as a grasshopper, went to a giant, and prayed him to lend
her a sack. The giant consented, and even graciously offered to accompany her, at which she
expressed her extreme delight. The fairy, after
walking by the side of such a huge creature, had,
no doubt, swelled herself into a tolerable bulk,
for, on arriving at Bacharach, she took the sleeping barbers, one by one, and placed them in the
sack; after which, she told the giant to put it
upon his back, and to take it away—that it did
not matter where it was placed. It being night,
the giant did not perceive what the old woman
had done; he obeyed her, and strode off with his
accustomed strides. The barbers of Bacharach,
heaped one over another, awoke, and began to
move in the sack. The giant, through fright, increased his pace. As he traversed the Reichenberg, one of the barbers, who had his razor in
his pocket, drew it out, and made so large a hole
in the sack that all the barbers fell out, screaming frightfully. The giant, thunderstruck, im-
agining that he had a nest of devils on his back,
saved himself by means of his enormous legs.
When the emperor arrived at Bacharach there
was not a barber in the place; and, on Beelze-
bub coming to see the deed performed, a raven,

perched upon the gate of the town, said to his grace the Devil—

"My friend, in the middle of your face you have something so large that you could not see it even in a looking-glass—that is, *un pied de nez.*"

Since that time there has been no barber at Bacharach ; and even to this day, it is impossible to find a shop belonging to one of the fraternity. As for those stolen by the fairies, they established themselves where they fell, and built a town upon the spot, which they called the "Barbers' Village." Thus it is that the Emperor Frederick the First preserved his beard and his surname.

Besides the Mouse, the Cat, the Lurley, the Swiss Valley, and the Reichenberg, there is also near St. Goar the once formidable castle that shook before Louis the Fourteenth, and crumbled under Napoleon,—the Rheinfels.

About a mile from St. Goar we perceive, at the side of two mountains, a handsome feudal town, with ancient streets, fourteen embattled towers, and two large churches of Gothic structure. It is Oberwesel, a town of the Rhine, which was often the seat of war. Its old walls exhibit innumerable holes, the effects of the cannon-ball. At present, Oberwesel, like an old soldier, has become a vine-dresser. The red wine here is excellent.

Like all other towns upon the Rhine, Oberwesel has near it a castle in ruins—Schoenberg;
where, in the tenth century, the seven laughing
and cruel girls lived, who were turned, in the
middle of the river, into seven rocks.

The road from St. Goar to Oberwesel is full of
attractions. It runs along the Rhine, which is at
times hidden from our view by hawthorn-trees
and willows. All here is still, all is tranquil,—
save at intervals, when the pervading silence is
broken by a silvery salmon leaping to catch its
prey.

In the evening, after we have taken one of
those delightful walks which tend to open the
deep caverns of the stomach, we return to St.
Goar, and find, at the top of a long table, surrounded by smokers, an excellent German supper, with partridges larger than chickens. We
recruit our strength marvelously; above all, if
our appetite be so good as to permit us to over-
look a few of the strange *rencontres* which often
take place on the same plate—for instance, a
roast duck with an apple pie, or the head of a
wild boar with preserves. Just before the supper
draws to a close, a flourish of a trumpet, mingling with the report of a gun, is suddenly heard.
We hurry to the window. It is the French
hussar, who is rousing from dormancy the echo
of St. Goar, which is not less marvelous than

that of Lurley. Each gunshot is equal to the
report of a cannon ; each blast of a trumpet
is echoed with singular distinctness in the profound darkness of the valley. It is an exquisite
symphony, which seems to be mocking while it
pleases us. As it is impossible to believe that
this huge mountain can produce such an effect,
at the expiration of a few minutes we become
dupes of illusion, and the most grave thinker
is ready to swear that in those shades, under
some fantastic thicket, dwells a solitary — a
supernatural being—a sort of fairy—a *Titania*,
who amuses herself by delicately parodying the
music of mortals, and throwing down the half
of a mountain every time she hears the report
of a gun. The effect would be still greater if we
could, for a short time, forget that we are at the
window of an inn, and that that extraordinary
sensation has served as an extra plate to dessert.
But all passes away very naturally ; the per-
formance over, a waiter belonging to the auberge
enters, with a tin plate in his hand, which he presents to the inmates. Then all is finished ; and
each retires after having paid for his *echo*.

7*

CHAPTER XVIII.

BACHARACH.

Furstemberg, Sonnech, and Heimberg.—Europe.—A Happy
Little World.—The Cemetery.

THIS is one of the oldest, the prettiest, and
the most unknown towns in the world. At
my window are cages full of birds; from the roof
of my room hangs an old-fashioned lantern; and
in the corner is a ray of the sun, imperceptibly
but gradually advancing towards an old oak
table.

I remained three days at Bacharach, which is,
without exception, the most antique group of
human habitations that I have ever seen. One
might imagine that some giant, a vender of *bric-
à-bac*, purposing to open a shop upon the Rhine,
had taken a mountain for his counter, and
placed, from the bottom to the top, with a giant
taste, heaps of enormous curiosities.

This old, fairy town, in which romance and
legend abound, is peopled by inhabitants who
—old and young, from the urchin to the grand-
father, from the young girl to the old dame
—have, in their cast of features and in their
walk, something of the thirteenth century.

From the summit of the Schloss we have an immense view, and discover, in the embrasures of the mountain, five other castles in ruins; upon the left bank of the river, Furstemberg, Sonnech, and Heimberg; to the west, on the other side of the Rhine, Goutenfels, full of re- collections of Gustave Adolphe; and, towards the east, above the fabulous valley of Wisper- thall, the manor, where the inhospitable Sibo de Lorch refused to open the door to the Gnomes on stormy nights.

At Bacharach a stranger is looked upon as a phenomenon. The traveler is followed with eyes expressive of bewilderment. In fact, no one, ex- cept it be a poor painter, plodding his way on foot, with a wallet upon his back, ever visits this antique capital—this town of melancholy.

I must not, however, forget to mention that in the room adjoining mine hangs a picture pur- porting to represent Europe. Two lovely girls, their shoulders bare, and a handsome young fellow, are singing. The following stanza is un- derneath:

> " Enchanting Europe! where all-smiling France
> Gives laws to fashion, graces to the dance:
> Pleasure, fine arts, each sweet and lovely face,
> Form the chief worship of thy happy race."

Under my window was an entire little world, happy and charming—a kind of court, adjoining a Roman church, which we could approach by a dilapidated stair. Three little boys and two little girls were playing among the grass, which reached their chins; the girls every now and then fighting voluntarily with the boys. The ages of all five could not amount to more than fifty years. Beyond the long grass were trees loaded with fruit. In the midst of the leaves were two scare-crows, dressed like Lubins of the Comic Opera; and although, perhaps, they had the effect of frightening the birds, they failed to do that to the *bergeronettes*. In all corners of the garden were flowers glittering in the rays of the sun, and round these flowers were swarms of bees and butterflies. The bees hummed, the children chattered, the birds sang, and at a little distance were two doves billing.

After having admired till night-fall this charming little garden, I took a fancy to visit the ruin of the old church, which is dedicated to St. Werner, who suffered martyrdom at Oberwesel. I reached the first flight of steps, which were covered with grass, looked round, admired the heavens, from which sufficient light came to enable me to see the old palatine castle in ruins; then my eyes fell upon my charming garden of children, birds, doves, bees, butterflies, and music —my garden of life, of love, and of joy,—and I discovered that it was a cemetery.

CHAPTER XIX.

"FIRE! FIRE!"

Lorch.—An Incident.—Combat of the Hydra and Dragon.—
The Hotel P—— at Lorch.

WHEN twelve strikes at Bacharach we go to bed—we shut our eyes—we try to dispel the thoughts of day—we come to that state when we have, at the same time, something awake, and something asleep—when the fatigued body reposes, and when the wayward mind is still at labor. When thus, between the mind and body we are neither asleep nor awake, a noise suddenly disturbs the shades of night—an inexpressible, a singular noise,—a kind of faint murmuring—at once menacing and plaintive, which mingles with the night wind, and seems to come from the high cemetery situated above the village. You awake, jump up, and listen. What is that? It is the watchman blowing his trumpet to assure the inhabitants that all is well, and that they may sleep without fear. Be it so; still, I think it impossible to adopt a more frightful method.

At Lorch a person might be awoke out of his

sleep in a manner still more dramatical ; but, my
friend, let me first tell you what sort of a place
Lorch is.

Lorch, a large borough, containing about
eighteen hundred inhabitants, is situated upon
the right bank of the Rhine, and extends as far
as the mouth of the Wisper. It is the valley of
legends,—it is the country of fairies. Lorch
is situated at the foot of the Devil's Ladder, a
high rock, almost perpendicular, which the valiant Gilgen clambered when in search of his betrothed, who was hidden by the gnomes on the
summit of a mountain. It was at Lorch that the
fairy Ave invented—so say the legends—the art
of weaving, in order to clothe her lover Heppius.
The first red wine of the Rhine was made here.
Lorch existed before Charlemagne, and it has
left a date in its charter as far back as 732.
Henry the Third, Archbishop of Mayence, resided here in 1348. At present there are neither
Roman cavaliers, nor fairies, nor archbishops ;
yet the little town is happy, the scenery is delightful, and the inhabitants are hospitable. The
lovely house of the Renaissance, on the border of
the Rhine, has a facade as original and as rich in
its kind as that of the French manor of Meillan.
The fortress, teeming with legends of old Sibo,
protects, as it were, the borough from the historical castle of Furstemburg, which menaces it

with its huge tower. There is nothing more
charming than to see this smiling little colony of
peasants prospering beneath those two frightful
skeletons, which were once citadels.

A week ago, perhaps it was about one in the
morning, I was writing in my room, when suddenly I perceived the paper under my pen
become red, and, on lifting my eyes, I discovered that the light did not proceed from my
lamp, but from my window, while a strange
humming noise rose around me. I hastened to
ascertain the cause. An immense volume of
flame and smoke was issuing from the roof above
my head, making a frightful noise. It was the
hotel P——, the house adjoining mine, which
had taken fire.

In an instant the inmates of the *auberge* were
awake, all the village was astir, and the cry of
"Fire! fire!" was heard in every street. I shut
my window, and opened the door. The large
wooden staircase of my hotel, which had two
windows, almost touched the burning house, and
seemed also to be in flames. From the top to
the bottom of the stairs, a crowd of shadows,
loaded with divers things, was seen pressing,
jostling, and making way, with all possible speed,
either to the top or to the bottom. It was the
inmates of the *auberge* removing their effects,—
one nearly naked, this one in drawers, that one

in his shirt; they seemed scarcely awake. No
one cried out—no one spoke. It was like the
humming of an ant-hillock.

As for me,—for each thinks of himself at such
a time,—I had little luggage. I lodged on the
first floor, therefore ran no other risk than that
of being forced to make my escape by the
window.

In the meanwhile, a storm arose, and the rain
came down in torrents. As it always happens,
the more haste the less speed. A moment of
frightful confusion ensued; some wished to
enter, others to go out: drawers and tables,
attached to ropes, were lowered from the windows; and mattrasses, nightcaps, and bundles
of linen, were thrown from the top of the house
on to the pavement. Women were wringing
their hands in despair, and children crying.
Just as the fire gained the granary, the fire-
engines arrived. It is almost impossible to give
an idea of the rage with which the water attacked its enemy. No sooner had the pipes
passed over the wall than a hissing sound was
heard; and the flames, on which a stream of
molten steel seemed pouring, roared, became
erect, leaped frightfully, opened horrible mouths,
and with its innumerable tongues, licked at once
all the doors and windows of the burning edifice.
The vapor mingled with the smoke, volumes of

which were dispersed with every breath of wind, and lost themselves, twisting and wreathing, in the darkness of the night, whilst the hissing of the water responded to the roaring of the fire. There is nothing more terrible and more grand than the awful combat of the *hydre* and *dragon*.

The strength of the water forced up in columns by the engines was extraordinary; the slates and bricks on which it alighted, broke and were scattered by its force. When the timber-works gave way the sight was grand. Amidst noise and smoke, myriads of sparks issued from the flames. For a few minutes a chimney-stack stood alone upon the house, like a kind of stone tower; but no sooner was the pipe pointed towards it than it fell heavily into the gulf. The Rhine, the villages, the mountains, the ruins—all the spectres of the country—were observable amidst the smoke, and flames, and storm. It was truly a frightful sight, yet it had something of sublimity in it.

If looked at in detail, nothing more singular than to see, at intervals, amongst smoke and flame, heads of men appearing everywhere. These men were directing the water-pipes on the flames, which jumped, advanced, and receded. Large blocks of wood-work were detached from the roof, and hung dangling by a nail, while others fell amidst noise and sparks.

In the interior of the apartments the decorated paper of the walls appeared and disappeared with every blast of the wind. There was upon the wall of the third floor a picture of Louis XV., surrounded with shepherds and shepherdesses. I watched this landscape with particular interest. For some time it withstood the fire; but at last one body of flame entered the room, stretched forth one of its tongues, and seized the *landscape ;*—the females embraced the males; Tircis cajoled Glycère; then all disappeared in smoke.

A short distance from the *auberge* was a group of half-naked English with pale countenances, and looks expressive of bewilderment. They were standing by the goods which had been providentially saved. On their left was an assemblage of all the children of the place, who laughed on seeing a block of wood precipitated into the burning element, and clapped their hands every time the water-works happened to play amongst them. Such was the fire of the hotel P——, at Lorch.

A house on fire is at best a house burning; but, what is still more melancholy, a man lost his life at it, while in the act of doing good to others.

About four o'clock in the morning the people became what is generally termed masters of the fire, and succeeded in confining the flames to the

Hotel P——, thus saving ours. A host of servants, brushing, scraping, rubbing, and sponging, attacked the rooms, and in less than an hour our inn was washed from top to bottom. One thing is remarkable—nothing was stolen! All the goods, removed in haste amidst the rain, in the dead of the night, were scrupulously carried back by the poor peasants of Lorch.

Next morning I was surprised to see, on the ground-floor of the inn that was burnt, two or three rooms perfectly entire, which did not seem to be the least disordered by the fire that had raged above them. *Apropos* of this fact, the following story passes current in this country.

A few years ago an Englishman arrived somewhat late at an inn at Braubach, supped, and went to bed. In the middle of the night the *auberge* took fire. The servants entered the apartment of the Englishman, and finding him asleep, awoke him, told him what happened, and that he must make all speed out of the house.

"To the d—l with you!" said the Englishman, not at all pleased with his nocturnal visitants. "You awake me for that! Leave me alone; I am fatigued, and will not get up! you seem to be a parcel of fools, to imagine that I am going to run through the fields in my shirt at such an hour as this! Nine hours is the amount of time that I allow for rest. Put out the fire the best way you can! As for me, I am very well in bed, where I intend to remain. Good night! I will see you to-morrow."

No sooner had he said so than he turned his back upon the servants, and fell fast asleep. What was to be done? The fire gained ground; and the inmates, to save themselves, fled, after shutting the door upon the Englishman, who was soundly sleeping, and snoring tremendously. The fire was terrible, but at last was, with great difficulty, extinguished. Next morning, the men who were clearing the rubbish came to the chamber of the Englishman, opened the door, and found him in bed. On perceiving them he said, yawning—

"Can you tell me if there is such a thing as a boot-hook in this house?"

He rose, breakfasted heartily, and appeared quite refreshed—a circumstance greatly to the displeasure of the lads of the place, who had made up their minds to make what is called in the valley of the Rhine a *bourgmestre sec* with the Englishman—that is a smoked corpse; which they show to strangers for a few liards.

CHAPTER XX.

FROM LORCH TO BINGEN.

LORCH is about four French leagues from
Bingen. You are well aware of my taste.
Whenever an opportunity is offered, I never
neglect converting my excursion into a promenade.

Nothing to me is more pleasing than traveling
on foot. We are free and joyous. No breaking down of wheels, no contingencies attendant
on carriages. We set out; stop when it suits us;
breakfast at a farm or under a tree; walk on,
and dream while walking—for traveling cradles
reverie, reverie veils fatigue, and the beauty of
the country hides the length of the road. We
are not traveling—we wander. Then we stop
under the shade of a tree, by the side of a little

rivulet, whose rippling waters harmonize with the songs of the birds that load the branches over our heads. I saw with compassion a diligence pass before me, enveloped in dust, and containing tired, screwed-up and fatigued passengers. Strange that those poor creatures, who are often persons of mind, should willingly consent to be shut up in a place where the harmony of the country sounds only in noise, the sun appears to them in clouds, and the roads in whirlwinds of dust. They are not aware of the flowers that are found in thickets, of the pearls that are picked up amongst pebbles, of the Houris that the fertile imagination discovers in landscapes!— *musa pedestris.* Everything comes to the foot-passenger. Adventures are ever passing before his eyes.

I remember being, some seven or eight years ago, at Claye, which is a few leagues from Paris. I will transcribe the lines which I found in my note-book, for they are connected with the story that I am going to relate.

"A canal for a ground-floor, a cemetery for a first, and a few houses for a second—such is Claye. The cemetery forms a terrace over the canal; thus affording the manes of the peasants of Claye a probable chance of being serenaded by the mail-packet which runs from Paris to Meaux."

I was returning to Paris on foot, and had set out early: the trees of the forest of Bondy tempted me to go by a road which had a sharp turning, where I seated myself—my back against an oak, my feet hanging over a ditch—and began to write in my green-book the note which you have just read. As I was finishing the fourth line I lifted my eyes, and perceived, not many yards from where I was, a bear, with its eye fixed upon me. In broad daylight we have no nightmares, nor can we be dupes enough to take the stump of a tree for something supernatural. At night, things may change in appearance; but at noon, with a May sun over our heads, we have no such hallucinations. It was actually a bear—a living bear—a hideous looking animal, which was seated on its hind legs, with its fore paws crossed over its belly. One of its ears was torn, as also was its under-lip: it had only one eye, with which it looked at me attentively. There was no woodman at hand—all around me was silent and deserted. I must say that I felt a strange sensation. Sometimes, when chance brings us into contact with a strange dog, we manage to get over the difficulty by shouting out " Fox," " Solomon," or " Asor;" but what could we say to a bear? Where did it come from? Why such a creature in the forest of Bondy, upon the high-way from Paris to Claye? It was strange, un-

reasonable, and anything but pleasing. I moved
not; I must also say that the bear did not move,
a circumstance which appeared to me somewhat
lucky. It looked at me as tenderly as a bear
could well do with one eye; it opened its mouth,
not in ferocity, but yawningly. This bear had
something of peace, of resignation, and of drow-
siness; and I found a likeness in its physiognomy to those old stagers that listen to trage-
dies. In fact, its countenance pleased me so
much that I resolved to put as good a face upon
the matter as I could. I therefore accepted it
for a spectator, and continued what I had begun.
I then wrote the fifth line in my book; which
line is at a considerable distance from the fourth,
for, on beginning it, I had my eyes fixed upon
the eye of the bear.

Whilst I was writing a large fly lighted on the
bleeding ear of my spectator. It slowly lifted its
right paw, and passed it leisurely over its ear, as
a cat might do. The fly took to its wings; the
bear looked after it: then he seized his hind legs
with his fore paws, and, as if satisfied with that
classic attitude, began again to watch me. I
admit that I observed his movements with no
slight degree of interest.

Just as I was about to begin the sixth line, I
heard a sound of feet on the high road, and suddenly I perceived another bear, a huge, black

animal, which had no sooner fixed its eyes upon the former than it ran up to it and rolled graciously at its feet. The first was a she-bear, and did not deign to look upon the black one; and fortunately the latter paid no attention to me.

I confess that at this new apparition, which was somewhat perplexing, my hand trembled. I was then writing, " *Claye, a probable chance of being serenaded.*" In my manuscript I see there is a great space between the words " *probable chance,*" and " *of being serenaded.*" That space signifies—" a second bear ! "

Two bears! What did all this mean? Judging from the direction the black one came, it was natural to imagine that it was from Paris; a city little abounding with *betes*, at least of such savage natures.

I remained petrified—bewildered—with my eyes fixed upon the hideous animals, which began to roll lovingly in the dust. I rose, and was making up my mind whether I should pick up my cane, which had fallen into the ditch, when another appeared, less in size, more deformed, and bleeding like the first ; then came a fourth, a fifth, and a sixth. The last four walked along the road like soldiers on the march. This was truly inexplicable. A moment afterwards I heard the shouting of men, mingling with the barking of dogs; then I beheld ten or twelve bull-dogs,

8

and seven or eight men : the latter armed with large sticks, tipped with iron, and carrying muzzles in their hands. One of them stopped, and, whilst the others collected and muzzled the animals, he explained to me this strange enigma. The master of the Circus of the Barrière du Combat, profiting by the Easter devotions, was sending his bears and dogs to Meaux, where he intended giving a few exhibitions. All these animals traveled on foot, and had been unmuzzled at the last stage, to afford them an opportunity of eating by the roadside. Whilst the keepers were comfortably seated in a neighboring *cabaret*, the bears, finding themselves alone, joyous of liberty, stole a march upon their masters.

Such was one of the adventures of my pedestrian excursions—the *rencontre* of " actors " on a half-holiday.

Dante, in the commencement of his poem, states that he met one day a panther in a wood ; after which, a lion ; then a bear. If we give credit to tradition, the Seven Wise Men of Greece had similar adventures. Thales, of Milet, was, for a long time, followed by a *griffon ;* Bias de Priene walked side by side with a lynx; Solon, of Athens, bravely confronted a mad bull; Cleobulus, of Rhodes, met a lion ; and Chilo, of Macedonia, a lioness. All these marvelous facts, if properly examined, might be found to have some connection with the "holiday" of a menagerie. If I had related my story of the bears in a manner more redounding to my valor, perhaps in a few hundred years I should have passed for a second Orpheus. *Dictus ob hoc lenire tigres.* You perceive, my friend, that poor "*acting*" bears give rise to many prodigies. Without offense to the ancient poets or Greek philosophers, I must confess that, to me, a strophe would be but a feeble weapon against a leopard, or the power of a syllogism against a hyena. Man has found the secret of degrading the lion and the tiger—of adding stupidity to ferocity. Perhaps it is well: for, had it not been so, I should have been devoured; and the Seven Wise Men of Greece would have shared the same fate.

Since my boyhood I have always derived extreme delight from traveling on foot, for in many of my pedestrian trips I have met with adventures which have left a pleasing impression behind.

The other day, about half-past five in the morning, after having given orders for my luggage to be transported to Bingen, I left Lorch, and took a boat to convey me to the other side of the river. If you should ever be here, do the same. The Roman and Gothic ruins of the right bank are much more interesting to the

traveler than the slate-roofed houses of the left.
At six I was seated, after a somewhat difficult
ascent, upon the summit of a heap of extinguished lava, which overlooks Furstemburg
Castle and the valley of Diebach. After view-
ing the old castle, which in 1321, 1632, and 1689,
was the seat of European struggles, I descended. I left the village, and was walking
joyously along, when I met three painters, with
whom I exchanged a friendly "good day."
Every time that I see three young men traveling
on foot, whose shining eye-balls reflect the fairy-
land of the future, I cannot prevent myself from
wishing that their chimeras may be realized,
and from thinking of the three brothers, Cade-
net, Luynes, and Brandes, who, two hundred
years ago, set out one beautiful morning for the
court of Henry IV., having amongst them only
one mantle, which each wore in turn. Fifteen
years afterwards, under Louis XIII., one of
them became Duke of Chaulnes; the second,
Constable of France; and the third, Duke of
Luxembourg! Dream on, then, young men—
persevere !

Traveling by threes seems to be the fashion
upon the borders of the Rhine, for I had scarcely
reached Neiderheimbach when I met three more
walking together.

They were evidently students of some of those

noble universities which tend so much to civilize
Germany. They wore classic caps, had long
hair, tight frock-coats, sticks in their hands,
pipes in their mouths, and, like painters, wallets
on their backs. They appeared to be conversing
with warmth, and were apparently going to
Bacharach. In passing, one of them cried out,
on saluting me—

"*Dic nobis domine, in qua parte corporis animam
veteres locant philosophi?*"

I returned the salutation, and replied, "*In corde
Plato, in sanguine Empedocles, inter duo supercilia
Lucretius.*"

The three young men smiled, and the eldest
shouted—"*Vivat Gallia regina!*" I replied,
"*Vivat Germania mater!*" We then saluted
each other, and passed on.

Above Neiderheimbach is the sombre forest
of Sann, where, hid among trees, are two
fortresses in ruins ; the one, that of Heimburg,
a Roman castle ; the other, Sonneck, once the
abode of brigands. The Emperor demolished
Sonneck in 1212; time has since crumbled Heimburg. A ruin still more awe-striking is hid
among the mountains—it is called Falkenburg.

I had, as I have already stated, left the village
behind me. An ardent sun was above, but the
fresh breeze from the river cooled the air around.
To my right, between two rocks, was the narrow

entry of a charming ravine, abounding with
shadows. Swarms of little birds were chirping
joyously, and in love chasing each other amongst
the leaves; a streamlet, swollen by the rains,
dashed, torrent-like, over the herbage, frightened
the insects, and, when falling from stone to stone,
formed little cascades among the pebbles. I discovered along this stream, in the darkness which
the trees shed around, a road, that a thousand
wild flowers—the water-lily, the amaranth, the
everlasting, the iris—hide from the profane and
deck for the poet. There are moments when I
almost believe in the intelligence of inanimate
things: it appeared to me as if I heard a thousand voices exclaim—

"Where goest thou? Seekest thou places
untrod by human foot, but where Divinity has
left its trace? Thou wishest thy soul to commune with solitude; thou wishest light and
shadow, murmurings and peace, changes and
serenity; thou wishest the place where the Word
is heard in silence, where thou seest life on the
surface and eternity at the bottom; thou lovest
the desert; thou hatest not man; thou seekest
the greensward, the moss, the humid leaves, tall
branches, birds which warble, running waters,
perfume mingling with the air. Well, enter:
this is thy way." It required no consideration. I entered the ravine.

To tell you all that I did there, or, rather, what solitude did for me—how the wasps buzzed round the violets, how the wings of birds rustled among the leaves—that which startled in the moss, that which chirped in the nest, the soft and indistinct sound of vegetation, the beauty of the bull-fly, the activity of the bee, the patience of the spider, the opening of flowers, the lamentations, the distant cries, the struggling of insect with insect, the exhalations of the rocks, which, sighingly, reached the ear—the rays of Heaven, which pierced through the trees,—the drops of water that fell, like tears, from flowers—the half revelations which came from the calm, harmonious, slow, and continued labor of all those creatures and of all those things which are more in connection with God than with man;—to tell you all that, my friend, would be to express the ineffable, to show the invisible, to paint infinity! What did I do there? I no longer know. As in the ravine of Saint Goarshausen, I wandered, ruminated: and, in adoring, prayed! What was I thinking of? Do not ask me. There are moments when our thoughts float as drowned in a thousand confused ideas.

I at last reached—I do not know how—the summit of a very high hill, covered with short broom. In all my excursions upon the banks of the Rhine, I saw nothing so beautiful. As far as

the eye could reach were prairies, waters, and
magic forests resembling bunches of green feathers. It was one of those places where we imagine we see the tail of that magnificent peacock
which we call Nature.

Behind the hill on which I was seated, on the
summit of a mount covered with fir and chestnut
trees, I perceived a sombre ruin, a colossal heap
of brown basalt, in the form of a citadel. What
castle was it? I could not tell, for I did not
know where I was. To examine a ruin at hand
is my *manie;* therefore, at the expiration of a
quarter of an hour, I was wandering through it,
searching, foraging, and turning over huge stones,
with the hope of finding an inscription which
would throw some light upon this venerable
ruin.

On leaving the lower chamber, the corner of a
stone, one end buried in the rubbish, struck my
view. I immediately stooped, and with my hands
and feet cleared everything away, under the impression of finding upon it the name of this mysterious ruin. On this large block of stone, the
figure of a man, clothed in armor, but without a
head, was sculptured, and under his feet were the
following lines :

"Vox Tacvit periit lux. Nox rvit et rvit vmbra vir
caret in tvmba qvo caret effigies."

I was still in ignorance. This castle was an

enigma. I had sought for words. I had found
them: that is, an inscription without a date—an
epitaph without a name—a statue without a
head. While buried in reflection, a distinct
sound of voices reached me. I listened. It was
a quick dialogue, a few words only of which I
could distinguish amid the shouts of laughter
and of joy. These were—"*Fall of the mountain
—Subterranean passage—Very bad footpath.*" On
rising from the tombstone, I beheld three young
girls, clothed in white, with fair faces, smiling
cheeks, and bright blue eyes. Nothing could be
more magical, more charming, for a *reveur*, so
situated, than this apparition. It would have
been pardonable for a poet to have taken them
for angels, or saints of Heaven; I must affirm
that, to me, they were three English girls.

It suddenly crossed my mind that by profiting by these angels I might find, without further
trouble, the name of the castle. They spoke
English; therefore, I concluded that they belonged to that country. To give me countenance, I opened my portfolio, called to my aid
the little English of which I was master, then
began to look into the ravine, murmuring to myself—"Beautiful view! Very fine! Very pretty
waterfall!" &c., &c.

The young girls, surprised at my sudden appearance, began, while stifling their laughs, to

8*

whisper to each other. They looked charming, but were evidently laughing at me. I summoned up courage, advanced a few steps towards the blooming group, which remained stationary, and saluting, with my most gracious air, the eldest of the three, uttered—

"What, if you please, is the name of this castle?"

The sweet girl smiled, looked at her two companions, and, slightly blushing, replied in French—

"I believe, Sir, it is called Falkenburg. At least, a French gentleman, who is now speaking with my father in the Grand Tower, said so. If you will take the trouble to go round that way, Sir, you will meet them." These words, so much to the point, and spoken with a pure French accent, sufficed to convince me of my mistake; but the charming creature took the trouble of adding—

"We are not English, Sir; we are French; and you are from France!"

"How do you know, Miss," I replied, "that I am a Frenchman?"

"By your English," the youngest replied.

The eldest sister looked at her with an air of severity—that is, if beauty, grace, youth, innocence, and joy, can have a severe air. For my part, I burst into a fit of laughter.

"But, young ladies," I said, "you, yourselves, were speaking English a few minutes ago."

"It was only for amusement," the younger replied.

"For exercise," said the other chidingly.

This flat and motherly rectification was lost upon the young girl, who ran gayly to the tombstone, raising slightly her gown, on account of the stones, and displaying the prettiest foot imaginable. "Oh!" she cried, "come and see this. It is a statue—it has no head—it is a man!"

The other two joined their sister; and a minute afterwards all three were upon the tomb, the sun reflecting their handsome profiles upon the granite spectre. A few minutes ago, I was asking myself the names of these young girls; and I cannot tell you what I felt when seeing, thus together, these two mysteries, the one full of horror, the other full of charms.

By listening to their soft whisperings, I discovered the name of the second. She was the prettiest—a true princess for fairy tales. Her long eyelashes half hid the bright apple of her eye, that the pure light penetrated. She was between her younger and her elder sister, as *pudeur* between naiveté and grace, bearing a faint resemblance to both. She looked at me twice, but spoke not; she was the only one of the three whose voice I had not heard, and the only one whose name I knew. At one time her younger sister said to her—"Look, Stella!" I at no former period so well understood all that is limpid, luminous, and charming in that name.

The youngest made these reflections in an audible voice:—"Poor man! they have cut his head off. It was then the time when they took off the heads of men!" Then she exclaimed— "O! here's the epitaph. It is Latin: 'VOX TACUIT PERIIT LUX.' It is difficult to read. I should like to know what it says."

"Let us go for father," said the eldest; "he will explain it to us." Thereupon all three bounded away like fawns. They did not even deign to ask me; and I was somewhat humbled on thinking that my English had given them a bad opinion of my Latin. I took a pencil, and wrote beneath the inscription the following translation of the distich:

> Dans la nuit la voix se tue,
> L'ombre éteignit le flambleau.
> Ce qui manque à la statue
> Manque à l'homme en son tombeau.

Just as I was finishing the last line I heard the young girls shouting—"This way, father—this way!" I made my escape, however, before they appeared. Did they see the explanation that I

had left them? I do not know. I hastened to
a different part of the ruin, and saw them no
more. Neither did I hear anything further of
the mysterious decapitated chevalier. Sad destiny! What crimes had that miserable man committed? Man had bereft him of life; Providence
had added to that forgetfulness. His statue was
deprived of a head, his name is lost to legends,
and his history is no longer in the memory of
man! His tombstone, also, will soon disappear.
Some vine-dressers of Sonneck, or of Rupertsberg, will take it, and trample upon the mutilated skeleton that it perhaps still covers, break
the stone in two, and make a seat of it, on which
peasants will sit, old women knit, and children
play. In our days, both in Germany and France,
ruins are of utility; with old palaces new huts
are constructed.

But, my friend, allow me to return to Falkenburg. It is enough for me, in this nest of legends, to speak of this old tower, still erect and
proud, though its interior be dilapidated. If you
do not know the adventures that transpired here
—the legends that abound respecting this place
—a recital of a few of them may amuse you.
One in particular,—that of Gantram and Liba,—
starts fresh in my memory. It was upon this
bridge that Gantram and Liba met two men carrying a coffin; and on this stair that Liba threw

herself into her lover's arms, saying smilingly,—
"A coffin! No, it is the nuptial bed that you
have seen!" It was in this court, at present
filled with hemlock, in flower, that Gantram,
when conducting his bride to the altar, saw—to
him alone visible—a man clothed in black, and a
woman with a veil over her face, walking before
him. It was in this Roman chapel, now crumbling, where living lizards now creep upon those
that are sculptured, that, when Gantram was putting the wedding-ring upon the taper finger of
his bride, he suddenly felt the cold grasp of an
unknown hand—it was that of the maiden of the
castle, who, while she combed her hair, had sung,
the night long, near an open and empty grave.

I remained several hours in these ruins—a
thousand ideas crowded upon me. *Spiritus loci !*
My next chapter may contain them. Hunger also
came ; but, thanks to the French deer that a fair
voyageuse whom I met spoke to me about, I was
enabled to reach a village on the borders of the
Rhine, which is, I believe, called Trecktlings-
hausen—the ancient Trajani Castrum.

All that is here in the shape of an *auberge* is a
taverne à bière ; and all that I found for dinner
was a tough leg of mutton, which a student, who
was smoking his pipe at the door, tried to dis-
suade me from eating, by saying that a hungry
Englishman, who had been an hour before me,

had tried to masticate it, but had left off in dis-
gust. I did not reply haughtily, as Marshal de
Crequi did before the fortress of Gayi—" What
Barberousse cannot take, Barbegrise will take ;"
but I ate of the leg of mutton.

I set out as the sun was declining, and soon
left the Gothic chapel of St. Clement behind me.
My road lay along the base of several mountains.
on the summits of which were situated three castles—Reichenstein, Rheinstein (both of which
were demolished by Rodolph of Habsburg, and
rebuilt by the Count Palatine, and Vaugtsberg,
inhabited in 1348 by Kuno of Falkenstein, and
repaired by Prince Frederick of Prussia). My
thoughts turned upon a ruin that I knew lay between the place where I was and Bingen—a
strange, unsightly ruin, which, between the conflux of the Nahue and the Rhine, stands erect in
the middle of the river.

I remember from childhood a picture that
some German servant had hung above my bed :
it represented an old, isolated, dilapidated tower,
surrounded with water; the heavens above it
were dark, and covered with heavy clouds. In
the evenings, after having offered up my prayers
to God, and before reposing, I looked attentively
at the picture. In the dead of the night I saw
it in my dreams, and then it was terrible. The
tower became enormous, the lightning flashed

from the clouds, the waters roared, the wind whistled among the mountains, and seemed every moment as if to pluck them from their base. One day I asked the servant the name of the tower, and she replied, making the sign of the cross upon her forehead—"Mausethurm." Afterwards she told me the following story :

"At one time there lived at Mayence a cruel archbishop named Hatto—a miserly priest—who, she said, was "readier to open his hand to bless, than to bestow in charity." That one bad harvest he purchased all the corn, in order to sell it again at a high price ; money was the sole desire of this wicked priest. That at length famine became so great that the peasants in the villages of the Rhine were dying of hunger—that the people assembled in the town of Mayence, weeping, and demanding bread—and that the archbishop refused to give them any. The starving people did not disperse, but surrounded the palace, uttering frightful groans. Hatto, annoyed by the cries of starvation, caused his archers to seize the men and women, old and young, and to shut them up in a granary, to which he set fire. "It was," added the old woman, "a spectacle that might have caused the stones to weep." Hatto did nothing but laugh, and as the wretched sufferers were screaming in agony, and were expiring in the flames, he exclaimed :

"Do you hear the squeaking of the rats?"

The next day the fatal granary was in ashes, and there were no longer any inhabitants in Mayence. The town seemed dead and deserted; when suddenly a swarm of rats sprang—like the worms in the ulcers of Assuérus—from the ashes of the granary, coming from under the ground, appearing in every crevice, swarming the streets, the citadel, the palace, the caves, the chambers, and the alcoves. It was a scourge, an affliction, a hideous *fourmillement*. Hatto, in despair, quitted Mayence, and fled to the plains, but the rats followed him; he shut himself up in Bingen, which was surrounded by walls, but the rats gained access by creeping under them. Then the despairing bishop caused a tower to be erected in the middle of the Rhine, and took refuge in it; the rats swam over, climbed up the tower, gnawed the doors and windows, the walls and ceilings, and, at last, reaching the palace, where the miserable archbishop was hid, devoured him. At present the malediction of Heaven and of man is upon this tower, which is called Mausethurm. It is deserted—it is crumbling into ruins in the middle of the stream; and sometimes at night a strange red vapor is seen issuing from it resembling the smoke of a furnace:—it is the soul of Hatto, which hovers round the place.

There is one thing remarkable. History, occasionally, is immoral; but legends are always moral, and tend to virtue. In history the powerful prosper, tyrants reign, the wicked conduct themselves with propriety, and monsters do well; a Sylla is transformed into an honorable man; a Louis the Eleventh and a Cromwell die in their beds. In tales, Hell is always visible. There is not a fault that has not its punishment—not a crime, which leads not to inquietude—no wicked men but those who become wretched. Man, who is the inventor of fiction, feels that he has no right to make statements and leave to vague supposition their consequences; for he is grouping in darkness—is sure of nothing; he requires instruction and counsel, and dares not relate events without drawing immediate conclusions. God, who is the originator of history, shows what he chooses, and knows the rest.

Mausethurm is a convenient word, for we may find in it whatever we desire. There are individuals who believe themselves capable of judging of everything, who chase poesy from everything, and who say, as the man did to the nightingale—"Stupid beast! won't you cease to make that noise." These people affirm that the word Mausethurm is derived from *maus* or *mauth*, which signifies "*custom-house ;* that in the tenth century, before the bed of the river was enlarged, the Rhine had only one passage, and that the authorities of Bingen levied, by means of this tower, a duty upon all vessels that passed. For these *grave* thinkers—these wise-acres—the cursed tower was a *douane*, and Hatto was a custom-house officer.

According to the old women, with whom I freely associated, Mausethurm is derived from *maus*, or *mus*, which signifies a *rat*. The pretended custom-house is the Rat Tower, and its toll-keeper a spectre.

After all, these two opinions may be reconciled. It is not altogether improbable, that towards the sixteenth and seventeenth century, after Luther, after Erasmus, several burgomssters of nerve made use of the tower of Hatto for a custom-house. Why not? Rome made a custom-house of the temple of Antonius, the *dogana*. What Rome did to History, Bingen might well do to Legend.

In that case *Mauth* might be right, and *Mause* not be wrong.

Let that be as it may, one thing is certain—that since the old servant told me the story of Hatto, Mausethurm has always been one of the familiar visions of my mind. You are aware that there are no men without their phantoms, as there are none without their whims.

Night is the time of dreams; at one time a

ray of light appears, then a flame of fire ; and, according to the reflection, the same dream may be a celestial glory, or an apparition of hell.

I must admit that the Rat Tower, in the middle of its agitated waters, never appeared to me but with a horrible aspect. Also—shall I avow it ?—when chance, by whose fantasy I was led, brought me to the banks of the Rhine, the first thought that struck me was, not that I should see the dome of Mayence, or the Cathedral of Cologne, or the Poalz, but that I should see the Rat Tower.

Judge then of my feelings, poor believing poet and infatuated antiquary that I am ! Twilight slowly succeeded day ; the hills became sombre, the trees dark, and a few stars twinkled in the heavens. I walked on, my eyes fixed on obscurity ; I felt that I was approaching Mausethurm, and that in a few minutes that redoubtable ruin, which to me had, up to this day, been only a dream, was about to become a reality.

I came to a turn in the road, and suddenly stopped. At my feet was the Rhine, running rapidly and murmuring among the bushes ; to my right and left, mountains, or rather huge dark heaps, whose summits were lost in a sky in which a star was scarcely to be seen ; at the base, for the horizon, an immense curtain of darkness : in the middle of the flood, in the distance, stood a large black tower, of a strange form, from which a singular red light issued, resembling the vapor of a furnace, casting a glare upon the surrounding mountains, showing a mournful-looking ruin on the left bank, and reflecting itself fantastically on the waters. There was no human voice to be heard; no, not even the chirping of a bird. All was solitude—a fearful, and sad silence, troubled only by the monotonous murmurings of the Rhine.

My eyes were fixed upon Mausethurm. I could not imagine it more frightful than it appeared. All was there—night, clouds, mountains; the quivering of the reeds; the noise of the flood, full of secret horror, like the roaring of hydras under water; the sad and faint blasts of wind; the shadows, abandonment, isolation; all, even to the vapor of the furnace upon the tower —the soul of Hatto!

An idea crossed my mind, perhaps the most simple, but which at that moment produced a giddiness in my head. I wished at that hour, without waiting till next day, or till daylight, to go to the ruin. The apparition was before my eyes, the night was dark, the phantom of the archbishop was upon the tower. It was the time to visit Mausethurm.

But how could I do it? where could I find a boat in such a place? To swim across the Rhine would be to evince too great a taste for spectres. Moreover, had I imagined myself a good swimmer, and been fool enough for such an act, the redoubtable gulf of Bingerloch, which formerly swallowed up boats as sea-dogs swallow herrings, and which is at this identical spot, would have effectually deterred me. I was somewhat embarrassed.

Continuing my way towards the ruin, I remember that the tinkling of the silver bell and the spectres of the dungeon of Velmich did not prevent the peasants from propping the vine and exploring the ruins; I concluded that near a gulf, where fish necessarily abound, I should probably meet with the cabin of some fisherman. When vine-dressers brave Falkenstein and his Mouse, fishermen might well dare Hatto and his Rats.

I was not deceived. I continued, however, walking for some time before I met anything; but at length reached a point of the bank where the Nahue joins the Rhine. I began to give up all hopes of meeting a waterman, but on descending towards some osiers, I descried a boat of a strange construction, in which a man, enveloped in a covering, was sleeping. I went into the boat, awoke the man, and pointed to the tower; but he did not understand me. I then showed him one of the large Saxony crowns, which are of the value of six francs each: he understood me immediately; and a few minutes afterwards, without exchanging a word, we, spectre-like, were gliding towards Mausethurm.

When in the middle of the flood, it seemed to me as if the tower diminished in size, instead of increasing.

It was the Rhine which made it appear less. As I had taken the boat at a place which was higher up than Mausethurm, we descended the river, advancing rapidly. My eyes were fixed upon the tower, from the summit of which the vague light was still issuing, and which, at each stroke of the oar, I saw distinctly increasing. Suddenly I felt the bark sinking under me, as if we were in a whirlpool, and the jerk caused my stick to roll at my feet. I looked at my companion, who, returning my gaze with a sinister smile, which, seen by the supernatural light of Mausethurm, had something frightful in it, said "Bingerloch." We were upon the gulf. The boat turned. The man rose, seized the anchor with one hand and a cord with the other, plunged the former into the surge, leaped on the gunwale, and began to walk upon it. This manœuvre was accomplished with admirable dexterity and marvelous *sang-froid*.

We landed. I raised my eyes. A short distance from where I stood, on a little island not observable from the land, was Mausethurm, an enormous formidable castle, dilapidated and in fragments, as if gnawed by the frightful rats of the legend.

The faint light that I observed was a red flame which shed rays along the mountains, giving to every crevice the appearance of the mouth of an enormous lantern. It also seemed to me as if I heard in that fatal edifice, a strange continued noise—a sort of gnawing sound.

I looked at the waterman, told him to wait my return, and walked towards the ruin.

It was truly the tower of Hatto—the place of rats. Mausethurm was before my eyes, and I was about to enter. In directing my steps towards a low door in the facade, through which the wind from the river was whistling, I was startled by some black living creature, which ran rapidly by my feet. It appeared to me to be a huge rat running towards the reeds. On reaching the door, I ventured to look into the room, from which the strange gnawing sound and the extraordinary glare of light still came. I will tell you what I saw:

In an angle opposite the door were two men with their backs turned to me. One was in a stooping posture, and the other seated upon a kind of iron vise, which a person of discernment

might have taken for an instrument of torture.
Their feet and arms were naked, their clothes
tattered, and each wore a leathern apron. One
was old—his grey hair testified it; the other was
young—I saw his fair locks, which, from the reflection of a large, lighted furnace in the opposite angle, appeared red. The old man wore,
like the Guelphs, his cowl inclined to the right;
and the young one, like the Gibelins, had his
upon the left side. But they were neither Gibelins nor Guelphs, demons nor spectres. Two
blacksmiths were before me. The light—the soul
of Hatto, changed by Hell into a living flame—
was the fire and smoke of the chimney! the
gnawing sound, the sound of files!

The two blacksmiths were worthy individuals.
They showed me the ruins; pointed out the
place in which Hatto had taken shelter; and
then lent me a lantern, with which I ranged
through the whole of the little island.

After having examined the ruin, I left Mausethurm. My waterman was fast asleep, but was
no sooner roused than we proceeded forthwith to
cross the Rhine, when I again heard the noise of
the two blacksmiths.

Half an hour aftewards I arrived at Bingen;
was very hungry; supped: after which, although
fatigued, although the inhabitants were asleep in
their beds, I explored the Klopp, an old castle in

o

ruins which overlooks Bingen, where I witnessed a spectacle worthy of closing a day on which I saw so many things, with so many ideas crossing my mind.

CHAPTER XXI.

LEGEND OF THE HANDSOME PECOPIN AND THE BEAUTIFUL BAULDOUR.

The Planet Venus and the Bird Phœnix.—The Difference between the Ear of a Young Man and that of an Old one. —The Qualities Essential to Different Embassies.—Happy Effect of a Good Thought.—The Devil is Wrong in being a Gourmand.—Amiable Proposition of an Old Sage.—The Wandering Christian.—The Danger to which we Expose Ourselves by Getting on a Strange Horse.—The Return.— Bauldour.

I PROMISED to relate one of the legends of Falkenburg, perhaps the most interesting—that of the grave adventure of Guntram and Liba; but, after reflection, I think it would be useless to do so, as you will find it in almost any collection, written in a spirit far more enlivening than I could tell it. However, I will record one, which will be found nowhere else. You may thank the old French soldier for it. This follower of the republican army believes, at present, in gnomes and fairies, as devotedly as he formerly credited the *puissance* of the emperor. Solitude has always this effect upon the mind; it develops the poetry which is inherent in man,

and makes him a believer in the wonderful and
supernatural.

LEGEND OF THE HANDSOME PECOPIN AND THE BEAUTIFUL BAULDOUR.

The handsome Pecopin loved the beautiful
Bauldour, and the lovely Bauldour was enamored
of the gay Pecopin.   He possessed all the qualities of a lord and of a man; and she was a queen
when at home, a holy virgin at church, a nymph
in the woods, and a fairy at work.

Pecopin was an excellent hunter, and Bauldour
was a good spinster.   When he was absent, the
distaff amused and consoled her; and when the
sound of the horn, mingling with the noise of
the hounds, would strike her ear, she fancied she
could distinguish the words—"Think of thy
lover."   Besides, the wheel, which caused the
belle reveuse to stoop, was ever saying in a soft
and small voice—"Think of him."

When the husband and lover are united in one
person, all goes well.   Marry, then, the spinster
to the hunter, and fear nothing.

However, I must say that Pecopin was too
fond of hunting.   When he was on horseback,
the falcon resting on his hand, or when he was
following the stag, he forgot everything.   Whoever loves horses and dogs too much, displeases

woman; and he who loves woman too much displeases God. Govern, therefore, your tastes, and
bridle your inclinations.

When Bauldour, that noble and lovely young
girl, that star of love, of youth and of beauty,
saw Pecopin caressing his dog, a huge animal,
with large nostrils, long ears, and a black mouth,
she was jealous of it. She entered her room disconcerted and sad, and there wept. Then she
scolded her servants, and after them her dwarf.
Woman's anger is like rain in a forest—it falls
twice. *Bis pluit.*

In the evening Pecopin, blackened with pow-
der and weary with fatigue, returned to Bauldour, who pouted and murmured, with a tear in
the corner of her large, black eye. Pecopin
pressed her little hand, and she ceased murmuring; then he kissed her rosy lips, and she smiled.
She never suffered the chevalier to take her by
the waist. One evening he slightly pressed her
elbow, and her face colored up with blushes and
offended pride. She was betrothed and not married. Modesty in woman is what bravery is in
man.

PART II.

THE BIRD PHŒNIX AND VENUS.—Pecopin
had in his hall at Sonneck a large gilt painting,
which represented the nine heavens, each with

its appropriate color and name affixed to it :—
Saturn, leaden color ; Jupiter, clear and brilliant ;
Venus, the east on fire ; Mercury, sparkling ; the
Moon, with its silvery appearance ; the Sun,
shining flames. Pecopin erased the word Venus,
and substituted Bauldour.

The fair demoiselle had in her room large
tapestries, on which was an immense bird, the
size of an eagle, with a golden neck and a blue
tail. Above this marvelous animal was written
the Greek word " Phœnix." Bauldour effaced it,
and substituted " Pecopin."

The day fixed for the nuptials drew near.
Pecopin was full of joy, and Bauldour was
happy.

A week before the appointed day of marriage,
Bauldour was busily spinning at her window.
Her dwarf came to tell her that Pecopin was
coming up stairs, at which intelligence she rose
hurriedly to run to her betrothed, but her foot
got entangled with the thread, and she fell. Poor
Baldour rose ; she was not hurt, but remembering
that a similar accident happened at the castle to
Liba, she felt sad at heart. Pecopin entered
beaming with joy, spoke of their marriage and
of their happiness, and the cloud that hovered
round her soul vanished.

PART III.

THE DIFFERENCE BETWEEN THE EAR OF A YOUNG MAN AND THAT OF AN OLD ONE.— Next day Bauldour was spinning in her chamber, and Pecopin was hunting in the woods. He had no companion but his dog. In following the chase, he came to the forest of Sonn, where there are four large trees, an ash, an elm, a fir, and an oak—which are called by the people "*The Evangelists.*" As Pecopin passed under the shade, four birds were perched upon the trees—a daw upon the ash, a blackbird upon the elm, a magpie upon the fir, and a crow upon the oak. These feathered creatures made a strange, confused noise, and seemed as if they were interrogating each other. A few steps further on, an old man was seated on the stump of a tree ; and as Pecopin passed he turned round and said :

"Sir chevalier, do you know what the birds are saying?"

"My good fellow, Pecopin replied, "what does it matter to me?"

"Sir," said the peasant, "for the young the blackbird whistles, the magpie chatters, and the raven croaks ; for the old, the birds speak."

The chevalier burst out into a fit of laughter, saying, "Pardieu! you're raving."

"You are wrong, Sir Pecopin," said the old man, gravely.

"You never saw me before; how is it that you know my name?"

"From the birds," replied the peasant.

"You are an old fool, my worthy fellow," said Pecopin, continuing his route.

About an hour afterwards Pecopin heard the sound of a horn, and then perceived the Count Palatine and his suite, who were out on a hunting excursion.

"Holla!" one of them cried out, on seeing Pecopin, "my brave hunter—won't you accompany us?" He consented, and conducted himself so marvelously, by killing the different animals they pursued, that the count gave him a fief of Rhineck, enrolled him amongst his followers, and prevailed upon him to go to Stahleck, to take the oath of allegiance. Pecopin sent a message to Bauldour, announcing the intention of the pfalzgraf. "Be not uneasy, my beloved," he added; "I will be with you next month." The messenger set out, and Pecopin retired with the prince and his followers to the castle at Bacharach.

PART IV.

QUALITIES ESSENTIAL TO DIFFERENT EM-

BASSIES.—Pecopin was a nobleman by blood, by nature, and by outward appearance, and pleased the pfalzgraf so much, that this prince one day said to him : " My friend, I have an embassy for my cousin of Bourgogne, and your noble appearance and gallant behavior have induced me to make you my ambassador."

Pecopin obeyed the wishes of his prince, and went to Dijon, where the Duke received him kindly ; and he was soon after, on account of his rank, sent on an embassy to the King of France. One day the king said : " Pecopin, I require a gentleman to go to Spain on urgent business ; but, finding none of my followers capable of undertaking such a task, I have fixed upon you, on account of your mien and mind." Pecopin again set out ; and when the negotiation was terminated he went to the sultan to take his leave.

" I receive your adieus with pleasure, for you must set out immediately for Bagdad."

" For Bagdad ! " Pecopin replied, with astonishment.

" Yes, chevalier," replied the Moorish prince, " for I cannot sign the treaty with the King of France without the consent of the Caliph of Bagdad."

Pecopin went to Bagdad, where a strange adventure happened to him. One day, while pass-

9*

ing the walls of the seraglio, the sultan's favorite perceived him; and as he was handsome, bold, and of a haughty air, she conceived a passion for him and sent a black slave to speak to him—

"This talisman," she said, "is the gift of a princess who loves you, but who will never see you more. Take care of it, for as long as you wear it you will never be old; when you are in dangers touch it and you will be saved." Pecopin accepted the talisman, and attached it to his neck-chain. "Now," the slave added, "do not lose it, for whilst you have it in your possession, you will always have the same youthful appearance; but when you lose it, the infirmities of every year which has passed over your head will instantly attack you. Adieu, handsome giaour." Having said this the negress left him.

The caliph had observed his favorite's slave speaking with Pecopin, and was fired with jealousy. He invited the stranger to a feast, and at night conducted him to the summit of a high tower. Pecopin, without suspicion, advanced near the parapet, which was very low, when the caliph addressed him in these words:—

"Chevalier—the Count Palatine sent you to the Duke of Bourgogne on account of your renown; the Duke of Bourgogne sent you to the King of France because you were of a noble race; the King of France sent you to the Sovereign of Grenada on account of your wit; and he sent you to the Caliph of Bagdad because you were dignified in appearance. As for me, on account of thy fame, thy rank, thy wit, and thy fine appearance, I send thee to the Devil."

On pronouncing the last word, the caliph pushed Pecopin over the parapet.

PART V.

GOOD EFFECTS OF A GOOD THOUGHT.— When a man falls from a height, terrible ideas flash across his brain—life, which he is going to leave; and the regions of death, which he is about to enter. In that awful moment Pecopin thought of Bauldour—put his hand to his heart, and, without knowing, touched the talisman. No sooner had his finger come in contact with the magic stone, than he felt as if he were supported with wings. He no longer fell—he flew, and continued to do so all night. Just as day was breaking, the invisible hand that supported him placed him gently upon the seashore.

ART VI.

THE DEVIL IS WRONG IN BEING A GOUR-MAND.—At this time a singular and disagreeable adventure happened to the Devil. It was customary for Asmodeus to go about picking up all the souls that belonged to him, putting them into a bag and carrying them away upon his back. One day, being more fortunate than usual, he was filling his sack gayly, when, turning round, he beheld an Angel, who was smiling at him. The Devil shook up the bag, and continued filling for some time. At last he stopped, and seized hold of it to swing over his shoulder; but the souls that he had crammed into it were so numerous, and the iniquities with which they were burdened weighed so heavily, that he could not move it. He took both his hands, and made a second attempt, which proved as futile as the first. "O souls of lead!" the Devil exclaimed, and then he began swearing. Again he looked up, and he saw the Angel laughing at him.

"What are you doing there?" cried the Demon.

"You see well enough; I was smiling a short time ago; now I am laughing."

"O, celestial fowl! huge innocent! begone!" Asmodeus cried.

The Angel looked at him gravely, and said :—

"Hear me, Dragon; thou wilt not be able to carry away that load of souls till a saint from Paradise or a Christian from Heaven falls upon the earth and helps thee to put it on thy shoulders." That said, the Angel opened his wings and flew away.

The Devil was very much disconcerted. "What does that imbecile mean?" he muttered between his teeth. "A saint from Paradise, or a Christian from Heaven! I shall be forced to remain a long time if I wait the coming of such assistance. How, in the name of all the saints, did I so cram my sack."

As the Devil stood by the side of his heavy burden, heaping imprecations upon himself for his own stupidity, he cast his eyes upwards, and perceived a black speck in the heavens, which every moment became larger and larger. The Devil put his hands on his knees to take a better view of it, and discovered that it was a man— an armed Christian, bearing a cross upon his breast, falling from the clouds.

"What is it to me who sends him?" exclaimed the Devil, jumping with joy; "I am saved! I could not get over four saints a short time ago, who laughed at the pitiful tale that I told them; but it will be easy for me to manage this fellow."

Pecopin, on finding himself on *terra firma*, looked round, and on perceiving the old man, who was like a slave resting by the side of his load, he accosted him thus: "Who are you, friend? and, pray, where am I?"

The Devil whined out piteously—

"You, Sir, are on the borders of the Red Sea, and I am the most wretched of all miserable beings. I have a very cruel master, who has taken it into his head to build a mountain, and he obliges me, an old man, to carry loads of sand from the borders of the sea. I begin at the break of day, and never leave off before sunset. Yesterday I was returning with my sixth load, when fatigue overcame me. I thought I would rest myself, and afterwards found that I had not strength to lift the load on my shoulders, and therefore was obliged to remain here all night, looking at my burden, and cursing my master for his cruelty. My good Sir, for pity's sake help me up with this load, that I may return to my master. I am sure he will kill me."

Pecopin shook his head, saying, "Good man, your story is an unlikely one."

"My dear Sir," the Devil replied, "what has happened to you if told, would be as unlikely; yet it is true. Then," he continued, "what harm would it do to you to help an infirm old man to place his load upon his back?"

This was a just demand. Pecopin stooped, seized the bag, and was placing it on the back of the old man, who was leaning forward to receive the load. The Devil is vicious—it was for vice that he fell; he was greedy, which passion often causes the loss of all. The idea struck him of adding the soul of Pecopin to the others; but first of all he must kill Pecopin.

The Devil began to speak to some invisible spirit, in a kind of jargon, half Italian, half Spanish, which Pecopin fortunately understood:

"*Bamus, non ciera occhi, verbera, frappa, y echa la piedra.*"

Suspicion flashed like lightning across the the mind of Pecopin; he raised his eyes, and saw above his head an enormous stone that some invisible hand held suspended in the air.

He stepped backwards, touched his talisman with his left hand, seized his poniard with his right, and plunged it violently into the bag. The Devil cried hideously, and the souls, profiting by the hole which Pecopin had made, flew away, leaving behind them their dark deeds and crimes, which, by their natural attraction to the demon, fixed upon his back; thus it is that the Devil is always represented with a hump.

At the moment that Pecopin stepped backwards, the invisible giant dropped the stone, which fell upon the foot of the Devil, and crushed it; and from that day Asmodeus has always been club-footed.

The Devil, like Jove, has thunder at his command, but it is of a more frightful nature, coming from the earth and uprooting trees. Pecopin felt the ground tremble beneath him; a dense cloud rose around, and a noise met his ear: it appeared to him that he fell, and rolled along the earth like a withered leaf when blown by the wind. He fainted.

PART VII.

AMIABLE PROPOSITIONS OF AN OLD SAGE.— When Pecopin recovered, he heard a soft voice saying, "*Phi sma,*" which is Arabian, and signifies "He is in Heaven." Another person placed his hand upon his chest, and replied, "*Lo, lo, machi mouth,*" which means "No, no, he is not dead." Pecopin opened his eyes, and saw an old man and a young girl kneeling by his side: the countenance of the former was as dark as night; he had a long, white beard, and was enveloped in a scarf of green silk; the young girl was of a copper color, had large, hazel eyes, lips of coral, and gold rings hanging from her nose and ears. She was exceedingly handsome.

Pecopin was no longer by the seaside. The blast of Hell had borne him into a valley filled with rocks and trees of a strange form. He rose. The old man and the handsome female looked at him affectionately. He approached one of the trees; the leaves contracted, the branches receded, and the flowers, which were pale white,

became red. Pecopin recognized the mimosa, or
" tree of shame," and concluded that he had left
India, and was now in the famed country of
Pudiferan.

The old man beckoned to Pecopin to follow,
and in a few minutes all three were seated npon
a mat in a cabin built of palm-leaves, the interior
of which was filled with precious stones, that
shone like a heated furnace. The old man looked
at Pecopin, and said in German—

" My son, I am the man who knows everything—the great Ethiopian lapidary, the *taleb* of
the Arabs. I am the first that ever penetrated
this desert; thou art the second. I have passed
my life in gleaning from nature the science of
things, and filling them with the science of the
soul. Thanks to me and to my lessons; thanks
to the rays which, in this valley of animate stone,
of thinking plants, and of wise animals, have
fallen for a hundred years from my eyeballs! It
was I who pointed out to beasts their true medi-
cine, of which man stands so much in need. Till
now I have only had beasts for disciples, but have
long wished for a man. Thou art come; then be
my son. I am old. I will leave thee my cabin,
my precious stones, my valley, and my science.
Thou shalt marry my daughter, who is called
Aissab, and who is good and beautiful. We
shall pass our days happily in picking up

diamonds and eating the roots of plants. Be
my son."

"Thanks, my venerable seignor," Pecopin said;
"I accept with joy your kind offer."

When night came he made his escape.

PART VIII.

THE WANDERING CHRISTIAN.— To tell all the
adventures of Pecopin would be to relate the
voyage of the world.   At one time he was walking with naked feet on the sea-shore; at another,
in sandals, climbing a mountain; now riding upon
an ass,—afterwards seated on a zebra or an ele-
phant.   He lost in the desert, like Jerome Cos-
tilla, four of his toes; and, like Mendez Pinto,
was sold twenty times.   He clambered up mountains whose summits were hidden in the clouds,
and, on approaching their tops, vomited blood
and phlegm.   He came to that island which no
one when seeking can find, and to which chance
only can bring one.   In Scythia he killed a grif-
fin which the people had long been endeavoring
to destroy, in order to possess the gold guarded
by that animal; for which act they wished to
make him their king, but he declined their offer.
Amidst all his adventures, all his daring deeds,
his miseries, and troubles, the brave and faithful
Pecopin had only one end in view—to find Ger-

many—to enter Falkenburg, with the hope of seeing Bauldour.

He counted with a sad heart the days as they passed, and, on reaching the north of France, found that five years had elapsed since he had seen Bauldour. He sat down upon a stone by the roadside; his thoughts wandered to his beloved; something fell upon his hand; he started—it was a tear that had dropped from his cheek.

"Five years," he thought, "is a long time; but I will see her now." Then, though his feet were lacerated with the stones, and his clothes torn, he proceeded with a light heart on his journey.

After traveling all day among rocks, trying to discover a passage which descended to the Rhine, he arrived at a wood, which, without hesitation, he entered; and after walking for upwards of an hour, found himself near a ditch. Tired, and dying of hunger and thirst, he sank down upon the grass, lifted his eyes upwards, and perceived a flock of sheldrakes soaring above him.

In agony of soul, he was asking himself where he was, when the sound of some one singing in the distance floated on the evening breeze. Pecopin raised himself on his elbow, listened attentively, and distinguished these words:

Mon petit lac engendre, en l'ombre qui l'abrite,
La riante Amphitrite et le noir Neptunus ;
Mon humble étang nourrit, sur des monts inconnus,
L'empereur Neptunus et la reine Amphitrite,
　　Je suis le nain, grand-père des géants.
　　Ma goutte d'eau produit deux océans.

Je verse de mes rocs, que n'effleure aucun aile,
Un flueve bieu pour elle, un fleuve vert pour lui,
J'épanche de ma grotte, ou jamais feu n'a lui,
Le fleuve vert pour lui, lr fleuve bleu pour elle.
　　Je suis le nain, grand-père des géants.
　　Ma goutte d'eau produit deux océans.

Unc fine émeraude est dans mon sable jaune.
Un pur saphir se cache en mon humide écrin.
Mon émeraude fond et devient le beau Rhin ;
Mon saphir se dissout, ruisselle et fait le Rhone.
　　Je suis le nain, grand-père des géants.
　　Ma goutte d'eau produit deux océans.

Pecopin could no longer doubt the sad conviction that crossed his mind. Poor, hungry, and fatigued traveler! he was in the fatal Wood of the Lost Path, which is full of labyrinths, and where the dwarf Roulon is ever seen deceiving the traveler, who, if once within the wood is never known to leave it.

The voice was that of Roulon; the song was that of the wicked dwarf of the Bois des Pas Perdus.

Pecopin, in despair, threw himself on the ground, crying—"Alas! all is over. I shall never more behold Bauldour."

"You are wrong, if you serve me," said some one from behind.

Pecopin looked up, and beheld an old gentleman equipped for the chase. It was not the dwarf Roulon, which circumstance made his heart leap with joy.

"What do you want with me?" Pecopin demanded.

"To take thee to Bauldour," replied the old man, smiling.

"When?"

"After you have spent a night in the chase."

"But I am dying with hunger," Pecopin replied. "I am not able to get on horseback."

The old gentleman took a bottle from his pocket and presented it to Pecopin, who no sooner swallowed two or three mouthfuls than he felt invigorated, and cried—

"To the chase with all my heart. But shall I really see Bauldour to-morrow?"

"Before the sun rises you shall be at the gates of Falkenburg."

"Hollo, gentlemen! hollo!" the old man cried, "To the chase!"

On turning round, Pecopin perceived that his companion was humpbacked; and when he walked, he discovered that he was club-footed.

At the call of the old man a host of gentlemen, clothed like princes, and mounted like kings, came from a thicket, and ranged themselves round him. He seemed to be their master. All were armed with knives and spears, the old man alone having a horn. The night was dark; but suddenly two hundred servants appeared carrying torches.

"*Ebbene*," said the master, "*ubisunt los perros?*"

This mixture of Italian, Latin, and Spanish was not at all agreeable to Pecopin.

The old man then said with impatience—

"The dogs! the dogs!" and in less than a minute a pack came howling and barking to the spot.

Pecopin thought there was something extraordinary in all that he saw, and was beginning to consider whether he should follow in the chase, when the old man addressed him—

"Well, chevalier, what do you think of our dogs?"

"My good Sir," Pecopin replied, "to follow such animals we must have most wonderful horses."

The old man without replying, raised the horn to his mouth and blew it; a noise was heard among the trees, and two magnificent horses, black as jet, appeared.

"Well, seigneur," said the old man, smiling, "which of the two do you prefer?"

Pecopin did not reply, but leaped upon one of them. The old man asked him if he was well

saddled ; and, on being answered in the affirmative, he burst into a fit of laughter, jumped like a
tiger upon the other, which trembled fearfully,
and began to blow the horn so violently, that
Pecopin, deafened with the noise, believed that
this singular individual had thunder in his chest.

PART IX.

THE DANGER TO WHICH WE EXPOSE OUR-
SELVES BY GETTING ON A HORSE THAT WE DO
NOT KNOW.—At the sound of the horn a thousand strange lights started up in the forest ;
strange shadows were seen everywhere ; and the
words, " To the chase," were heard mingling
with the barking of the dogs, the neighing of
horses, and the shaking of the trees. Pecopin's
horse, accompanied by that of the old man,
started off at a violent gallop, making every step
resound in the lover's brain, as if the horse's
hoofs had come in contact with his skull. It
was a gallop, rapid, supernatural, which almost
deprived him of reason, for he was only sensible
to the frightful noise around—the whistling of
the wind, the rustling of leaves, the barking and
howling of dogs, and the neighing of horses.

Suddenly all was silent, save the sonnd of
the old man's horn in the distance. Pecopin
knew not where he was. He looked round, and

perceived his reflection in what he thought was
the White Lake, then in the Black one; but saw
it as the swallows see their shadows while gliding
over the surface of a pond.   In the midst of this
course he raised his hand to his talisman, and
suddenly he was enveloped in darkness, while his
horse began to gallop with renewed fury.   At
this terrible moment Pecopin commended his
soul to God, and his heart to his mistress.   He
continued for some time thus, flying, as it were,
through the air, when the thought struck him
that death was preferable to such torment.   He
tried to throw himself from his horse, but he
discovered that some iron hand held him by the
feet.

The distant cries, the barking of dogs, the
neighing of horses, mingling with the blasts of
the old man's horn, again resonnded frightfully
in his ears.   The poor chevalier closed his eyes
and resigned himself to his fate.   When he
opened them, the heat of a tropical night struck
his countenance! the roarings of tigers and lions
reached his ear; and he saw huge ruins and
strange trees.   Pecopin was in an Indian forest—
he again shut his eyes.

Suddenly his horse stopped, the noise ceased,
and all was quiet.

Pecopin, who had remained for some time with
his eyes shut, opened them, and found himself

before the facade of a sombre and colossal edifice.

The old man's horn resounded through the building, the doors of the castle opened violently, as if by a blast of wind, and Pecopin, on his horse, entered a magnificent room, splendidly lighted. He cast his eyes towards the extremity of the hall, and saw a number of guests, of strange appearance, seated at table. No one spoke; no one ate; nor did any of them look at him. There was an empty seat at the head of the table, which indicated that they were waiting their superior's arrival.

Pecopin discovered among this motley group the giant Nimrod; King Mithrobusane; the tyrant Machanidas; the Roman Consul, Æmilius Barbula the Second; Rollo, King of the sea; Zuentibold, the unworthy son of the great Arnolphe, King of Lorraine; Athelstan, King of England; Aigrold, King of Denmark. By the side of Nimrod, Cyrus, the founder of the Persian empire, was seated, leaning on his elbow.

The old man's horn was again heard; a large door, opposite the one by which Pecopin had entered, opened, and innumerable valets appeared, carrying an immense golden plate, in the middle of which was a stag with sixteen horns, roasted and smoking. The old man entered and took his seat; and after observing the

10

grave looks of his guests, burst into a fit of laughter, saying—

"*Hombres y mugeres, or ca vosotros belle signore domini et dominæ, amigos mios, comment va la besogne.*"

"You come very late," said one of the guests.

"That is because I have a friend that is fond of hunting; I wished to show him one of our excursions."

"Yes; but look," Nimrod said, pointing to a little crevice which exposed the break of day.

"Well, we must make haste," the old man said, making a sign to the valets to approach and deposit their load upon the table. Pecopin at this moment drew his sword, sunk his spurs into the sides of his horse, which moved forward, and said with a loud voice—

"*Pardieu!* whoever ye may be—spectres, demons, or emperors—I forbid ye to move; or, by all that is holy, you shall feel, as well as that old man, the weight of a living cavalier's sword upon the heads of phantoms. I am in the cave of shadows; but I shall do things real and terrible. Thou hast lied, miserable old man. Defend thyself; or, by the mass, I will cleave thy head, wert thou King Pluto in person."

"What's the matter, my dear Sir?" the old man replied, smiling. "You are going to sup with us."

The grimace which accompanied this gracious invitation exasperated Pecopin, who cried—

" Defend yourself, old villain! You made me a promise, and you shall pay dearly for breaking it."

" Ho, ho, my worthy friend! I have not done so ; you must wait a little."

"Thou promisedst to take me to Bauldour; thou knowest that she is my betrothed."

"Well, since you will have it, be it so. Bad examples are shown by males and females above to those below. The sun and moon are wedded, but they are a disconsolate couple, for they are never together."

"A truce to raillery!" Pecopin cried, bursting with rage, "or I will exterminate thee and thy demons, and purge thy cavern."

The old man replied, laughing, "Purge, my friend. Here is the prescription—senna, rhubarb, and Epsom salts."

Pecopin in fury leveled a blow at the old man's head, but his horse drew back, trembling. At this moment a gleam of light stole through a crevice, the cock crowed, and all disappeared. Pecopin, on his horse gliding from beneath him, found himself standing, sword in hand, in a ravine near an old castle. Day broke ; he lifted his eyes, and leaped with joy. It was the castle of Falkenburg. He sheathed his sword, and was beginning to walk cheerfully towards the manor, when he heard some one say :

"Well, Chevalier de Sonneck, have I kept my word?"

Pecopin turned round, and saw the little hunchback that he had met in the wood, who in irony asked him if he knew him. Pecopin said that he did, and thanked him for thus bringing him to his Bauldour.

"Wait a little," the old man said. "You were in too great a hurry in accusing me; you are in too great a hurry in returning me thanks. Listen. You are my creditor; I owe thee two things—the hump on my back and my clubfoot; but I am a good debtor. I found out thy inclinations, and I thought it would be a pity to debar such a good hunter as thou art from partaking in the night chase."

Pecopin involuntarily shuddered, and the Devil added :

"If thou hadst not had thy talisman, I would have taken charge of thee ; but I am as well pleased that things have turned out as they have done."

"Tell me, demon," Pecopin said ; "is Bauldour dead, or married, or has she taken the veil?"

"No;" the demon replied, with a sinister grin.

"She is at Falkenburg, and still loves me?"

"Yes."

"In that case," Pecopin said, respiring as if a load had been taken from his chest, "whoever thou art, and whatever may happen, I thank thee."

"Dost thou?" the Devil replied. "Then, if thou art satisfied, so am I." On saying these words, he disappeared.

Pecopin shrugged his shoulders, and said to himself, smilingly:

"Bauldour lives; she is free, and still loves me. What have I to fear? When I met the demon yesterday evening, five years had expired since I left her, and it is now only a day more."

He approached the castle, recognized with joy each projection of the bridge, and felt happy. The threshold of the house in which our boyish have been spent, like the countenance of an offectionate mother, smiles upon us, when returning after a years' absence, with all the vigor of manhood.

As he was crossing the bridge, he observed a beautiful oak, whose top overlooked the parapet. "That is strange," he said to himself; "there was no tree there." Then he remembered that, two or three week before he left, Bauldour and he had amused themselves by throwing acorns at each other, and that at this spot one had fallen into the ditch.

"The Devil!" he exclaimed: "an acorn be-

come a tall oak in five years! this is certainly a
fertile soil !"

Four birds were perched upon this tree, trying
which could make the most noise. Pecopin
looked up, and saw a daw, a blackbird, a magpie,
and a crow; he hurried on—his thoughts were
on Bauldour.

He arrived at the staircase, and was ascending
quickly, when he heard some one laughing behind him, but on turning round, could see nothing. He reached the door, in which was the
key; his heart beat violently; he listened, and
the sound of a wheel struck his ear. Was it
that of Bauldour? Pecopin, trembling, turned
the key, opened the door, entered, and beheld
an old woman, decrepid and worn down by age,
her face covered with a thousand wrinkles, long
grey hair, escaping here and there from her cap,
her eyebrows white, and gums toothless. This
venerable, yet frightful object was seated near
the window, her eyes fixed upon the wheel at
which she was spinning, with the thread betwixt
her long thin fingers.

The old lady was apparently very deaf, for,
notwithstanding the noise that Pecopin made in
entering, she did not move. Nevertheless, the
chevalier took off his hat, as it becomes a man
before a person of advanced age, and, going near
her. said. " Madame, where is Bauldour?"

The old dame lifted her eyes, and fixed them on Pecopin; the thread dropped from her trembling hand; she screamed, and said with a feeble voice—

"Oh Heaven!—Pecopin? What would you? Masses for your troubled soul? or why is it that, being so long dead, your shadow still walks abroad?"

"Pardieu! my good lady," Pecopin replied, laughing and speaking very loud, so that, if Bauldour was in the next room, she might hear him;—"Pardieu! I am not dead! It is not my ghost which stands before you. I am of good solid flesh and bone, and have come back, not to have masses said for my soul, but for a kiss from my betrothed, whom I love more than ever."

As he finished the last words, the old lady threw herself into his arms. It was Bauldour! The night-chase with the Devil had lasted a hundred years!

Pecopin, distracted, left the apartment, ran down stairs, crossed the court, flew to the mountain, and took refuge in the forest of Sonneck. Like a madman, he wandered about the woods all day: and when evening came, seeing that he was approaching the turrets of his own castle, he tore off the rich clothes which the Devil had given him, and threw them into the torrent of Sonneck. Suddenly, his knees trembled, his hands shook, and to prevent himself from falling, he leaned against a tree. In Pecopin's exccss of grief, he had unconsciously seized the talisman, and thrown it, with his clothes, into the torrent. The words of the Sultana's slave proved true. In one minute Pecopin had all the infirmities attendant upon extreme old age. At that moment, he heard a burst of laughter; he looked round, but could see no one.

Pecopin, in pain and dejection, supporting himself on a stick, was returning to his castle, when he perceived a jackdaw, a blackbird, a magpie, and a crow, seated on the roof of the out-house. He remembered the words of the old man — "For the young the blackbird whistles, the magpie chatters, and the crow croaks, the hens cackle, and the doves coo; for the old man, the birds speak." He listened attentively, and the following is the dialogue he heard:—

BLACKBIRD.—Enfin mon beau chasseur, te voilà de retour.
JACKDAW.—Tel qui part pour un an croit partir pour un jour.
CROW.—Tu fis la chasse à l'aigle, ou milan, ou vautour.
MAGPIE.—Mieux eut value la faire au doux oiseau d'amour!
HEN.—Pecopin! Pecopin!
DOVE.—Bauldour! Bauldour! Bauldour!

CHAPTER XXII.

BINGEN.

Houses at Bingen. — Paradise Plain. — The Klopp. — Mdlle. Bertin.—The Sage.

BINGEN is an exceedingly pretty place, having at once the sombre look of an ancient town, and the cheering aspect of a new one. From the days of Consul Drusus to those of the Emperor Charlemagne, from Charlemagne to Archbishop Willigis, from Willigis to the merchant Montemagno, and from Montemagno to the visionary Holzhausen, the town gradually increased in the number of its houses, as the dew gathers drop by drop in the cup of a lily. Excuse this comparison; for, though flowery, it has truth to back it, and faithfully illustrates the mode in which a town near the conflux of two rivers is constructed. The irregularity of the houses—in fact everything, tends to make Bingen a kind of antithesis, both with respect to buildings and the scenery which surrounds them. The town, bounded on the left by the Nahue, and by the Rhine on the right, develops itself in a triangular form near a Gothic church, which is backed by a Roman citadel. In this citadel,

10*

which bears the date of the first century, and has long been the haunt of bandits, there is a garden; and in the church, which is of the fifteenth century, is the tomb of Barthélemy de Holzhausen. In the direction of Mayence, the famed Paradise Plain opens upon the Ringau; and in that of Coblentz, the dark mountains of Leyen seem to frown on the surrounding scenery. Here Nature smiles like a lovely woman extended unadorned on the greensward; there, like a slumbering giant, she excites a feeling of awe.

The more we examine this beautiful place, the more the antithesis is multiplied under our looks and thoughts. It assumes a thousand different forms; and as the Nahue flows through the arches of the stone bridge, upon the parapet of which the lion of Hesse turns its back to the eagle of Prussia, the green arm of the Rhine seizes suddenly the fair and indolent stream, and plunges it into the Bingerloch.

To sit down towards the evening on the summit of the Klopp,—to see the town at its base, with an immense horizon on all sides, the mountains overshadowing all—to see the slated roofs smoking, the shadows lengthening, and the scenery breathing to life the verses of Virgil—to respire at once the wind which rustles the leaves, the breeze of the flood, and the gale of the mountain—is an exquisite and inexpressible

pleasure, full of secret enjoyment, which is veiled
by the grandeur of the spectacle, by the intensity
of contemplation. At the windows of huts,
young women, their eyes fixed upon their work,
are gaily singing; among the weeds that grow
round the ruins birds whistle and pair; barks are
crossing the river, and the sound of oars splash-
ing in the water, and unfurling of sails, reaches
our ears. The washerwomen of the Rhine spread
their clothes on the bushes; and those of the
Nahue, their legs and feet naked, beat their linen
upon floating rafts, and laugh at some poor artist
as he sketches Ehrenfels.

The sun sets, night comes on, the slated roofs
of the houses appear as one, the mountains con-
gregate and take the aspect of an immense dark
body; and the washerwomen, with bundles on
their heads, return cheerfully to their cabins: the
noise subsides, the voices are hushed; a faint
light, resembling the reflections of the other
world upon the countenance of a dying man, is
for a short time observable on the Ehrenfels;
then all is dark, except the tower of Hatto,
which, though scarcely seen in the day, makes its
appearance at night, amidst a light smoke and
the reverberation of the forge.

A few days ago I was seated on the platform
at Klopp, and in a reverie had allowed my
thoughts to wander at freedom. Suddenly, a

small skylight window under my feet was opened, and I perceived a young girl appear at the window, who was singing to a slow and plaintive air, in a clear, rich voice, the following stanza:

> " Plas mi cavalier frances
>   E la dona catalana
>   E l'onraz del ginoes
>   E la court de castelana
>   Lou cantaz proveacales
>   E la danza trevisana
>   E lou corps aragones
>   La mans a kara d'angles
>   E lou donzel de Toscana."

I immediately recognized the joyful verses of Frederick Barberousse. It would be impossible for me to describe the effect they had upon me when heard in this ancient ruin, in the midst of obscurity—that song of the emperors, sung by a young girl; these Roman verses, accented by a German tongue; that gayety of by-gone times changed into melancholy; that ray of the Crusades piercing the shadow of the present, and throwing its light upon me, poor, bewildered dreamer.

Since I have spoken upon the music which I heard upon the Rhine, why not mention that which I heard when at Bacharach? Several students, seated upon the trunk of a tree, sang to German words that admirable air in " Quasimode," which is the most beautiful and most original in Mademoiselle Bertin's opera. The future, doubt it not, my friend, will render justice to that remarkable opera, which on its appearance was unfairly attacked and unjustly dealt with. The public, too often duped by ungenerous criticisms, by the malice of rivalry, with respect to works of genius, will think for itself, and will one day admire that soft and profound music, so pathetic and powerful, at moments melancholy, yet pleasing—music, so to speak, where, in each note, is mixed that which is most tender and most grave—the heart of a lady and the mind of a sage. Germany has already rendered her justice,—France will soon follow her example.

As I care little about what are termed local curiosities, I must admit that I did not see the miraculous horn, nor the nuptial bed, nor the iron chair of Broemser. To make amends, I visited the square dungeon of Rudesheim, the Roman caves, and saw lanterns of the thirteenth century and numerous sepulchral urns.

In the room where I was accustomed to dine at Bingen, I saw two individuals seated at opposite tables. There was such a contrast, both in their appearance and in their repast, that it could not fail to excite attention. The one was a huge Bavarian major, who spoke a little French, and who allowed dish after dish to be taken away without scarcely touching them; the other was a poor looking devil, seated before a plate of choucroute, who, after having his meagre pittance, finished his dinner by devouring with his eyes the loaded plates of his neighbor. The words of Albancourt struck me forcibly when looking at that living parable :—" *La Providence met voluntiers l'argent d'un coté et l'appetit de l'autre.*"

The poor fellow was a young *savant*, pale, grave, and melancholy. It was said that he was in love with one of the servants of the auberge, which is rather strange, for to me a *savant* in love is a problem. How is it possible that the studies, the dull experiments, and minute observations which compose the life of a sage, can agree with the hope, disappointment, jealousy, rage, and loss of time which attend the tender passion? Imagine how Doctor Huxham could have loved, who, in his excellent treatise " De Ære et Morbis Epidemicis," has told, month after month, the quantity of rain that fell at Plymouth during the period of twenty-two years. Imagine Romeo looking through a microscope, and counting the seventeen thousand *facettes* of the eye of a fly; Don Juan with an apron on, analyzing the *paratar trovinate* of potash; and Othello, in a stooping posture, looking for *gaillonelles* in the fossils of China.

However, in spite of all laws, this poor devil was in love. At times he spoke French, which was far superior to the major's, and his address was more gentlemanly—yet he had not a stiver. Sometimes my young savant drank, during the hours at table d'hote, a bottle of small beer, while his eye surveyed in envy the opening and shutting the mouths of the inmates of the hotel Victoria. The society here was rather mixed, and not at all harmonious. At the end of the table was an old English dame, and by her side three pretty children: she was apparently a governess or an aunt, whose consequential airs raised in my heart a feeling of sympathy for the pretty little ones. The major was seated near her, to whom, for politeness, he addressed his conversation, at one time describing an engagement, at another telling her he was going to Baden, because everybody went there. On his right hand was an advocate; and next to the advocate was an old man, whose thin gray hair and reverential mien had that mild appearance which a near approach to the grave gives, and which cites in every look the beautiful verses of Homer. In front of the old gentleman was my young sage, who spoke pompously of the "harrangues" that were brought from the sea. To me ".harens" (herrings) would have been more likely to have come from such a quarter.

One day I invited him to dine with me, which
invitation was cordially accepted—the more so,
perhaps, because the poor fellow had not breakfasted. We chatted a little, took a walk, and
afterwards visited the Island of Rats, which
pleased my companion very much; for a good
dinner, a gratuitous sail, and a chit-chat with the
worthy blacksmiths, were things which were not
of an everyday occurrence with him. Such were
my adventures at Bingen.

CHAPTER XXIII.

MAYENCE.

**Cathedral.—Its Interior.—Henry Frauenlob, the Tasso of May-
ence.—Market Place.**

MAYENCE and Frankfort, like Versailles
and Paris, may, at the present time, be
called one town. In the middle age there was a
distance of eight leagues between them, which
was then considered a long journey; now, an
hour and a quarter will suffice to transport you
from one to the other. The buildings of Frankfort and Mayence, like those of Liège, have been
devastated by modern good taste, and old and
venerable edifices are rapidly disappearing,
giving place to frightful groups of white houses.
I expected to see, at Mayence, Martinsburg,
which, up to the seventeenth century, was the
feudal residence of the ecclesiastical electors;
but the French made an hospital of it, which
was afterwards razed to the ground to make
room for the Porte Franc; the merchant's hotel,
built in 1317 by the famed League, and which
was splendidly decorated with the statues of
seven electors, and surmounted by two colossal

figures, bearing the crown of the empire, also shared the same fate. Mayence, however, though plunged into the *Renaissance*, possesses that which marks its antiquity—a venerable cathedral, which was commenced in 978, and finished in 1009. Part of this suberb structure was burnt in 1190, and since that period has, from century to century, undergone some change.

I explored its interior, and was struck with awe on beholding innumerable tombs, bearing dates as far back as the eighteenth century. Under the galleries of the cloister I observed an obscure monument, a bas-relief of the fourteenth century, and tried, in vain, to guess the enigma. On one side are two men in chains, wildness in their looks, and despair in their attitudes ; on the other, an emperor, accompanied by a bishop, and surrounded by a number of people, triumphing. Is it Barberousse? Is it Louis of Bavaria? Does it speak of the revolt of 1160, or of the war between Mayence and Frankfort in 1332? I could not tell, and therefore passed by.

As I was leaving the galleries, I discovered in the shade a sculptured head, half protruding from the wall, surmounted by a crown of flower-work, similar to that worn by the kings of the eleventh century. I looked at it: it had a mild countenance ; yet it possessed something of se-

verity in it—a face imprinted with that august
beauty which the workings of a great mind give
to the countenance of man. The hand of some
peasant had chalked the name "Frauenlob"
above it, and I instantly remembered the Tasso
of Mayence, so calumniated during his life, so
venerated after his death. When Henry Frauenlob died, which was in the year 1318, the females
who had insulted him in life carried his coffin to
the tomb, which procession is chiseled on the
tombstone beneath. I again looked at that noble
head. The sculptor had left the eyes open ; and
thus, in that church of sepulchres—in that cloister of the dead—the poet alone sees ; he only is
represented standing, and observing all.

The market-place, which is by the side of the
cathedral, has rather an amusing and pleasing
aspect. In the middle is a pretty triangular
fountain of the German *Renaissance*, which, besides having sceptres, nymphs, angels, dolphins,
and mermaids, serves as a pedestal to the Virgin
Mary. Upon one of the faces is the following
pentameter:

"Albertus princeps civibus ipse suis."

This fountain was erected by Albert de Braden-
burg, who reigned in 1540, in commemoration of
the capture of Francis the First by Charles the
Fifth.

Mayence, white though it be, receives not the respect of a mercantile city. The river here is not less crowded with sails, the town not less incumbered with bales, nor more free from bustle, than formerly. People walk, speak, push, sell, buy, sing, and cry; in fact, in all the quarters of the town, in every house, life seems to predominate. At night the buzz and noise cease, and nothing is heard at Mayence but the murmurings of the Rhine, and the everlasting noise of seventeen water mills, which are fixed to the piles of the bridge of Charlemagne.

CHAPTER XXIV.

FRANKFORT ON THE MAINE.

Jews at Frankfort. — Slaughter-House. — Roemer. — Inhabitants
of the Steeple.

I ARRIVED at Frankfort on a Saturday;
and after walking for some time in search
of the beauties of my old favorite town, I came
to a singular street, with two long ranges of
high, sombre, and sinister-looking houses, clinging to each other, as it were, with terror. Not a
door was open, not a window that was not secured with iron gratings. There was no singing,
no merry voices; no—a dismal silence reigned
over all. One or two men passed, who looked at
me with an air of suspicion and discontent, and
through the bars of iron of the third-floor windows I observed several females, whose countenances were of a brown color, and who looked
with stealth, to see who was passing. I was in
the street of the Jews; it was their Sabbath.

At Frankfort there are still Jews and Christians—true Christians who hate the Jews, and
Jews who hate the Christians.

Perhaps in no town in the world are there so

many statues and figures about the streets as
at Frankfort. Whichever way we turn, statues
of all epochs, of all styles, and of all sexes, are
sure to meet the eye; horned satyrs, nymphs,
dwarfs, giants, sphinxes, dragons, devils: in fact,
an unfortunate world of supernatural beings is to
be seen here.

One of the curiosities of Frankfort is the
Slaughter-house. It is impossible to see older
and blacker houses decorated with more splendid legs of mutton and loins of beef. Glut-
tonous and jovial-looking figures are curiously
sculptured upon the facades, and the openings
of the ground-floors seem like huge mouths,
ready to devour innumerable cattle, either living
or dead. The blood-bedaubed butcher chats
freely with the rosy-cheeked *bouchéres* under
garlands of gigots, and before a red stream, on
which two fountains are playing, as it runs smoking through the middle of the street. When I
was there, frightful cries was heard in all directions: it was a massacre of sucking-pigs that was
taking place. Servants, with baskets on their
arms, were laughing amidst the general uproar,
and casting amorous looks towards some stal-
wart youths, with knives in their hands, who
were ready to obey the demands of their cus-
tomers; here, some bargaining; there, others
quarreling. A butcher passed carrying a suck-

ing-pig by the hind legs, which I would have
purchased had I known what to do with it.
The poor little creature squeaked not; it was
ignorant of its impending fate, and knew not
what was about to take place. A pretty little
girl, about four years of age, was looking at it
with compassion; and seemed to beseech me
with her soft eyes to purchase the little thing
and save it from immediate death. I did not do
what that charming eye told me; I disobeyed
her demand, so sweetly expressed; but I re-
proached myself afterwards for not gratifying the
wishes of that innocent child.

After leaving the Slaughter-house, we enter
a large square, worthy of Flanders, and which
excites the curiosity of all travelers. It com-
prises all the styles of architecture of the Renaissance, and is ornamented according to the
taste of that epoch. Near the middle of the
square are two fountains—the one of the Renaissance, and the other of the eighteenth century, upon the tops of which are the statues of
Minerva and Judith, the Homeric and Biblical
viragos; the former bearing the head of Medusa,
the latter that of Holofernes.

Opposite this fountain is the Roemer, where
Emperors were proclaimed. I entered, and
wandered along a large hall with a long staircase, then amongst innumerable corridors. After

visiting the elector's hall, I came to the col-
legiate church of Frankfort, which is dedicated
to St. Barthélemy. The view here was charming. Over my head was a lovely sun; at my
feet, the town of Frankfort; to my left, the
Roemer; and to my right, the black and narrow
street of the Jews. Whilst buried in a profound
reverie, the clouds gathered above me, and,
chased by the wind, rolled about the heavens,
covering and uncovering at each instant shreds
of azure, while heavy drops of rain began to fall
upon the earth, and lightning to flash from the
heavens. I thought I was alone upon the tower,
and would have remained there all day, but suddenly a rustling noise startled me, and on looking round I perceived a young girl, about fourteen years of age, looking at me from a small
window. I advanced a few steps, and after passing the angle of the Pfarrthurm, I found myself
amongst the inhabitants of the steeple—a little
world, smiling and happy. A young girl was
knitting; an old woman, probably her mother,
spinning; doves were cooing on the top of the
steeple; and an hospitable monkey, on perceiving me, extended its little paw from the bottom
of its cage. Add to this the peace of elevated
places, where nothing is heard but the murmuring
of the winds, and from whence we see the beauty
of the surrounding country. In a part of the

tower the old woman had made a fire, on which she was cooking a humble repast. How this little family came there, and for what end, I do not know; but they interested me much. This proud city, once engaged in so many wars,— this city, which dethroned so many Cæsars,— this city, whose walls were like an armor, is at present crowned by the hearth of a poor old woman.

11

CHAPTER XXV.

THE RHINE.

Rafts on the Rhine.—Secret Souvenirs.—Oberwerth.

THE Rhine assumes all aspects—at one time broad, then narrow. It is transparent, tranquil, and rapid; it is a torrent at Schaffouse, a gulf at Laufen, a river at Sickingen, a flood at Mayence, a lake at St. Goar, and a marsh at Leyde.

The Rhine is calm, at least towards evening, and appears as if sleeping—a phenomenon more apparent than real, and which is visible upon all great rivers. The part of the Rhine the most celebrated and admired, the most curious for the historian, and the loveliest for the poet, is that which traverses, from Bingen to Kœnigswinter, that dark chaos of volcanic mounds which the Romans termed the *Alpes des Cattes*.

From Mayence to Bingen, as from Kœnigswinter to Cologne, there are seven leagues of rich smiling plains, with handsome villages, on the river's brink; but the great *encaissement* of the Rhine begins at Bingen by the Rupertsberg and Niederwald, and terminates at Kœnigswinter at the base of the Seven Mountains.

At each turning of the river, a group of houses — a town or borough — develops itself, with a huge tower in ruins peering over it. These hamlets present an imposing aspect; young women are seen busily washing and singing, with children playing round them; the basket-maker at work on the door-step of his hut; the fisherman mending his net in his boat; —all perform what God has ordered—man as well as the orb of day.

At the time of the Romans and of the Barbarians the Rhine was termed the "*street*" of soldiers; in the middle ages, when the river was bordered with ecclesiastical states, and, from its source to its mouth, was under the control of the Abbot of St. Gall, the Bishops of Constance, Bâle, Spire, Worms, the Archbishop-Electors of Mayence, Treves, and Cologne, the Rhine was called "the street of the priests;" at present it is that of the merchants.

The traveler who ascends the river sees it, so to speak, coming to him, and then the sight is full of charms. At each instant he meets something which passes him; at one time, a vessel crowded with peasants, especially if it be Sunday; at another, a steamboat; then a long, two-masted vessel laden with merchandise, its pilot attentive and serious, its sailors busy, with women seated near the door of the cabin ; here, a heavy-looking boat, dragging two or three after it ; there, a little horse, drawing a huge bark, as an ant drags a dead beetle. Suddenly there is a winding in the river; and formerly, on turning, an immense raft, a floating house, presented itself, the oars splash on both sides. On the ponderous machine were cattle of all kinds, some bleating, and others bellowing, when they perceived the heifers peaceably grazing on the banks. The master came and went, looked at this, then at that, while the sailors busily performed their respective duties. A whole village seemed to live on this float—on this prodigious construction of fir.

It is, perhaps, difficult to imagine such an island of wood coming and going from Namedy to Dordrecht, along the windings and turnings, the falls and serpentine meanderings of the Rhine. Wrecks, it is true, frequently take place, which gave rise to the saying, "that a float merchant ought to have three capitals—the first upon the Rhine, the second on land, and the third in his pocket." The conducting of each of these enormous constructions was left entirely to the charge of one man. At the end of the last century, the great *maitre flotteur* of Rudesheim was called "Old Jung." He died :

since that time these great floats have disappeared.

At present, twenty-five steamers are engaged on the Rhine, nineteen of which belong to the Cologne Steam Company, and are constantly plying from Strasburg to Dusseldorf; they are known by their white and black funnels. The remaining six belong to the Dusseldorf Company, which have tri-colored funnels, and ply from Mayence to Rotterdam. The ancient mode of navigating the Rhine, which was by vessels with sails, contrasts strangely with the present. The steamboats, with life in their appearance, rapid, comfortable, and painted with the colors of all nations, have for invocation the names of princes and cities: Ludwig II., Gross, Herzog von Hessen, Konigin, Victoria, Herzog von Nassau, Prinzessin Mariann, Gross Herzog von Baden, Stadt Manheim, Stadt Coblentz. The sailing vessels glide slowly along, and have at their prows grave and reverential names, such as Pius, Columbus, Amor Sancta Maria, Gratia Dei. The steamboat is varnished and gold lettered; the sailing vessel is bedaubed with pitch. The one pursues its way beseeching of men; the other continues its course in prayer. The one depends upon man; the other places its reliance in God—food, and that which is the gift of Heaven, being its cargo.

From Cologne to Mayence there are forty-nine
islands, covered with thick verdure, which hide
the smoking roofs, and shade the barks in their
charming havens, each bearing some secret *souvenir.* Graupenwerth, where the Hollanders
constructed a fort, and called it "the Priest's
Bonnet;" Pfaffenmuth, a fort which the Span-
iards took, and gave it the name of "Isabella;"
Graswerth, the island of grass, where Jean Philippe de Reichenberg wrote his "Antiquitates
Saynenses; Niederwerth, formerly so rich with
the gifts of the Margrave Archbishop, Jean II.;
Urmitzer Insel, which was well known to Cæsar;
and Nonnenswerth, the spot frequented by
Roland.

The souvenirs of the banks of the Rhine seem
to have responded to those of the islands, and
whatever took place on one side was sure to have
given rise to something else on the opposite one.
Permit me to run over a few of them. The coffin
of Saint Nizza, granddaughter of Louis-le-De-
bonnaire, is at Cologne; the tomb of Saint Ida,
cousin of Charles Martel, is at Cologne. Saint
Geneviéve lived in the woods at Fraunkirch, near
a mineral fountain, which is still seen, adjoining
a chapel that was built to her memory. It was
Schinderhannes who, with a pistol in his hand,
forced a band of Jews to take off their shoes;
then, after mixing them, ordered each person to

take the first pair he could find and be off, for he
would put the last to instant death. The terri-
fied Jews did so, and fled precipitately, some
stumbling, others limping and hobbling, making
a strange, clattering noise, which excited the
laughter of Jean l'Ecorcheur.

When the traveler has passed Coblentz, and
left behind him the graceful island of Oberwerth,
the mouth of the Lahn strikes his attention.
The sight here is admirable. The two crumbling
towers of Johanniskirch, which vaguely resemble
Jumeiges, rise, as it were, from the water's brink.
To the right, above the borough of Cappellan,
the magnificent fortress of Stolzenfels stands,
upon the brow of a huge rock; and to the left,
at the bottom of the horizon, the clouds and the
setting sun mingle with the sombre ruins of
Lahneck, which abound with enigmas for the historian, and darkness for the antiquary. On each
side of the Lahn is a pretty town, Niederlahn-
stein and Oberlahnstein, which seem smiling at
each other. A few stone-throws from the oriental
gate of Oberlahnstein, the trees of an orchard
disclose, and at the same time hide, a small
chapel of the fourteenth century, which is surmounted by a mean-looking steeple. The depo-
sition of Wencesles took place here.

In front of this chapel, upon the opposite
bank, is ancient Kœnigsstuhl, which, not more

than half a century ago, was the seat of royalty,
and where the emperors were elected by the
seven electors of Germany. At present, four
stones mark the place where it formerly stood,
After leaving this place, the traveler proceeds towards Braubach ; passes Boppart, Welmich, Saint
Goar, Oberwesel ; and suddenly comes to an immense rock, surmounted by an enormous tower
on the right bank of the river. At the base of
the rock is a pretty little town with a Roman
church in the center ; and opposite in the middle
of the Rhine is a strange, oblong edifice, whose
back and front resemble the prow and poop of a
vessel, and whose large and low windows are like
hatches and port-holes.

The tower is the Gutenfels ; this town is Caub ;
this stone ship—eternally on the Rhine, and
always at anchor—is the Palace, or Pfalz. To
enter this symbolic residence, which is built upon
a bank of marble, called "the Rock of the Palatine Counts," we must ascend a ladder that rests
upon a drawbridge, a portion of which is still to
be seen.

From Taunus to the Seven Mountains there
are fourteen castles on the right bank of the
river, and fifteen on the left, making in all twen-
ty-nine, which bear the *souvenirs* of volcanoes,
the traces of war, and the devastations of time.
Four of these castles were built in the eleventh

century—Ehrenfels, by the Archbishop of Sieg-
fried; Stahleck, by the Counts Palatine; Sayn,
by Frederick, first Count of Sayn, and vanquisher
of the Moors of Spain; and the others at a later
period.

This long and double row of venerable edifices,
at once poetic and military, which bear upon
their front all the epochs of the Rhine, every
one having its sieges and its legends, begins at
Bingen, by the Ehrenfels on the right, and by
the Rat Tower on the left, and finishes at
Kœnigswinter, by the Rolandseck on the left,
and the Drachenfels on the right.

The number which I have given only includes
those castles that are on the banks of the Rhine,
and which every traveler will see in passing; but
should he explore the valleys and ascend the
mountains, he will meet a ruin at every step;
and if he ascend the Seven Mountains, he will
find an abbey, Schomburg, and six castles—the
Drachenfels, Wolkenberg, Lowenberg, Nonnes-
tromberg, and the Œlberg, the last of which
was built by Valentinian, in the year 368.

In the plain near Mayence is Frauenstein,
which was built in the twelfth century, Scarfen-
stein and Greifenklau; and on the Cologne side
is the admirable castle of Godesberg.

These ancient castles which border the Rhine,
these colossal bounds, built by *Féodalité*, fill the

11*

country with reveries and pleasant associations.
They have been mute witnesses of bygone ages
—prominent features in great actions; and their
walls have echoed the cries of war and the murmurings of peace. They stand there like eternal
monuments of the dark dramas which, since the
tenth century, have been played on the Rhine.
They have witnessed, so to speak, monks of all
orders, men of all ranks; and there is not an
historical fact in the lives of those men who
took a prominent part on the Rhine that is not
designed on their venerable walls. They have
listened to the voice of Petrarch: they saw, in
1415, the eastern bishops. proud and haughty,
going to the assembly of divines at Constance,
to try Jean Huss; in 1441, going to the council
of Bâle, to depose Eugene IV.; and, in 1519,
to the diet of Worms, to interrogate Luther:
they witnessed, floating on the Rhine, the body
of Saint Werner, who fell a martyr to the Jews
in 1287. In fact, all the great events, from the
ninth to the nineteenth century, that transpired
on the banks of the flood have, as it were, come
under their notice. They are mute recorders of
the thing that were—of Pepin, of Charlemagne,
of Charles the Fifth, and of Napoleon. All the
great events which time after time, shook and
frightened Europe, have, like the lightning's
flash, lighted up these old walls. At present it

is the moon and the sun that shed their light upon these ancient edifices, famed in story and gnawed by time, whose walls are falling, stone by stone, into the Rhine, and whose dates are fast dwindling into oblivion.

O, noble towers! O, poor paralyzed giants! A steamboat filled with merchants and with peasants, when passing, hurls its smoke in thy faces.

INDEX.

INDEX.

A.

B.

C.

D.

PAGE

PAGE

H.

I.

See Hatto.

T.

V.

W.

Printed in the United States
206590BV00001BA/7/A

9 780898 758986